'Why' of Everything

"Why of Everything" is not about personal development.
It is about personal disruption.
Without personal disruption, personal growth is virtually impossible.

This SparkWise guide can show you how to harness the latest brain knowledge in your professional and personal life—every day.

Part 1

Colophon

Copyright © 2017	SparkWise B.V.
	Eddie Tjon Fo
	Marcel Bos
Cover design	Uma Brouwers
	Eddie Tjon Fo
	Marcel Bos
Illustrations	Raymond Bos
Photography	Eddie Tjon Fo
	Marcel Bos
Kindle edit	Melchior Bos
Final edit	Kiri Poananga
Photo location	Boutique Hotel
Amazon ISBN	9781973355243
Imprint	Independently published

All rights reserved. No part of this publication may be reproduced, distributed, or transmitted in any form or by any means, including photocopying, recording, or other electronic or mechanical methods, without the prior written permission of the publisher, except in the case of brief quotations embodied in critical reviews and certain other non-commercial uses permitted by copyright law.

For permission requests:
Mail publisher SparkWise directly, addressed "Attention: Permissions Coordinator", at office@sparkwise.nl

Quantity sales:
Special discounts are available on quantity purchases by corporations, associations, foundations and others. For details, contact the publisher at the address below.

Publisher: SparkWise Nederland B.V.
Diana Building, Herikerbergweg 292-342, 1101CT, Amsterdam, the Netherlands. office@sparkwise.nl

Social media

SparkWise	
	http://www.facebook.com/sparkwisenl
	http://www.twitter.com/sparkwisenl
Why of Everything	
	https://www.facebook.com/whyofeverything
	https://twitter.com/whyofeverything

First Edition

Dedication

We dedicate this book to our beloved families and wonderful friends, to our valued colleagues, advisory board, proofreaders, and the University of Life. We'd also like to use this opportunity to thank our dear clients for more than 20 years of loyalty.

We especially dedicate this book to our partners, for their endless patience, and for taking the time to read our manuscript over and over again, from the start of this book's journey, many years ago. We love you dearly.

We also dedicate this book, and its contents, to the personal disruption and ongoing development of each and every member of the human race on this little blue planet.

Acknowledgement

Our gratitude goes to our team of initial professional proofreaders.

Name	Profession
Ksenia Right	Speechwriter and international Presenter
Jasper Steffens	Entrepreneur and investor
Beryll Kraag	Fiscal Lawyer, writer and copywriter
Christine Sibilo	Entrepreneur, copywriter
John de Kok	Investor BrainCompass
Corinne Keijzer	Published Author
Rik Keijzer	Digital Marketer
Jeroen van der Graaf	Author, speaker and Tech Developer - Behavioral Scans
Pamela van Praag	Founder BRNDRZ
Nathalie Moser	Founder BRNDRZ

Interviews:
Joan Remmerswaal/CEO/Installation, Maintenance and Repair
Agnita Mur/Board Member/High School Education
Anja Loijens/Director of Operation/Hospitality Industry

Acknowledgement beta version readers

Ad Honders, Anita Boef, Anouska Bos, Farah El Baze, Fatima Perdijk, Fred van Slooten, Ilona Warris, Jeffrey Grootfaam, June Boldewijn, Kim de Nooij, Marco Mantel, Marya Yaqin, Melchior Bos, Nasra Bashe, Patriek Duismaker, Peter Blokland, Peter Hagedoorn, Raymond Bos, Roan Tjon Fo, Rutger van Drongelen, Sarah Pauwels, Ted Anema, Sjoerd Walinga, Sidney Cosman.

Tributes

I would personally like to thank Eddie and Marcel for their endless drive to finish this book. And so, a small word of honor for Marcel and Eddie.

Almost two years ago, when I was working on a disruptive Human Resources platform, I learned about two brain entrepreneurs working with several companies in Amsterdam to boost corporate performance, based on using brain laws. I was extremely motivated to meet up with Marcel and Eddie, and just listen to their story. I had red 'Spock pointed ears' after our first meeting.

Both Marcel and Eddie proved to be two well-seasoned entrepreneurs and managers, motivated to the bone to help start-ups to grow, and corporate companies to innovate. At first contact, I realized Marcel and Eddie have found a unique and powerful way to bring brain research into the corporate world, by offering hands on brain knowledge. Being motivated to learn from Marcel and Eddie, I took the decision to substantially invest in an extensive C-level brain course at their company SparkWise. The course gives you the knowledge to create a better version of yourself, and to build powerful harmony with your close friends, and within your working environment.

It does not answer all the high-level life questions we commonly share, but it instantly helps you to better understand all the interactions between you and the people around you.

Gaining in-depth knowledge of how the brains of 'us humans' function is the best present you can share with yourself and your loved ones, at any age.

I sincerely hope that the valuable and precious content of this book will help you, and many others like you, to improve your personal life, your business opportunities and your circle of close friends. It is also my hope that through their everlasting motivation, Marcel and Eddie continue to bring their knowledge into the world.

Guys, I just want to express my gratitude for the endless effort you have invested in converting the academic knowledge and shared content of this publication into a usable toolbox for everyday life. You just rock!

"More than ever, the power to adapt swiftly to a rapidly changing environment and optimal utilization of the available human capital within organizations determine the return on investment of any enterprise. Do not be afraid of new ideas that cause change, but just for the old methods and thinkers. Teach your brain to look for the causative side instead of the resultant side."

Jasper D. Steffens, Thunderminds.com

Word of Gratitude

I am very grateful to have been granted the opportunity to say a word of thanks and express my appreciation towards both Marcel and Eddie, for sharing their comprehensive knowledge of, and insights into, how the brain works. With this book, they have managed to explain how the brain functions in a way that helps you to understand, in many very recognizable—and sometimes hilarious—situations, why it is that you do what you do. It offers you the possibility to make the choice to acknowledge, and consequently use, this knowledge in a way that allows you to improve, quite literally, all aspects of your life.

For me, it would be presumptuous to state at this stage that the book has already resulted in a 180-degree change. I am, however, quite aware that after reading this book, a significant change in my life is imperative. Recognizing many of the situations described in the book, I have had more than just one aha moment. Reading about the apparent underlying reasons for my response (or more accurately: the response of my brain) to certain situations, was a true eye-opener. Therefore, the added value to me personally has been that the book has given me the tools to timely recognize those situations, and take appropriate actions accordingly. More concrete, it has helped me to recognize and acknowledge, work wise that is, where my passion actually lies.

As a result, I have chosen to shift my focus from activities I have been trained, and to some extent expected, to do, to activities that, deep down, I always knew I love to do. Even though I am at the very beginning of making this change in my life, it has already brought me an enhanced sense of profound contentment.

My sincere hope, therefore, is that this book will have the level of exposure, recognition and success it so very much deserves. Not only because it would be an excellent way to reward Marcel and Eddie for all the hard work they have done, and the many years spent conducting research, bringing into practice, and sharing what they know, but also because I honestly believe that reading this book will help people to materialize their dreams, and achieve success in all aspects, and at all levels, of their lives.

Marcel and Eddie, thanks again for your trust, in allowing me to be one of your proofreaders. Your knowledge about the brain is truly invaluable. Your translation of that knowledge into practical tools to tackle just about anything, in any situation that life throws at you, is simply priceless.

Beryll Kraag, Fiscal Lawyer.

Contents

Colophon 1
Dedication 3
Acknowledgement 4
Acknowledgement beta version readers 5
Tributes 6
Word of Gratitude 8
Contents 10
Foreword 15
What to expect from this book? 16
1. Have you ever wondered? 21
Why are we doing it wrong? 22
Building blocks 22
Biological DNA before you were born 23
World view up to 8 years old 24
Rules versus intrinsic motivation 25
The build of your personality 26
Brain laws and your professional mindset 26
Our intention with this book 28
2. Biological DNA 30
3. Brain school and brain knowledge 34
Brain school 34
Brain Knowledge 42
Differences between the male and female brain 44
4. Our perceptive truth versus the fMRI scanner 50

5. Primitive natural resistance 57
Fight, flight or freeze 57
Where does resistance come from 60
The hidden behavioral constraints which rule our emotions 61
How does the brain process external information? 63
Pain is 3 times stronger than happiness 64
Fear and negativity is contagious 68
The subconscious rules over our intelligence 69
Primary resistance is located in the subconscious 72
The urban jungle and stress 73
What is the effect of cortisol on our daily decisions 74
6. The hormone factory 76
Stress hormones creating negativity 78
Adrenaline 78
Noradrenalin 78
Cortisol 79
Hormones that produce happy or positive feelings 79
Endorphins 80
Dopamine 80
Serotonin 81
Oxytocin 82
7. The triune brain theory of Dr. Paul MacLean 84
Our brain stem or reptilian complex 85
The Limbic system 89
The buying button is located in the limbic system 95
The cortex/neocortex 98
8. A healthy brain 102
Negative influences on the brain 104

Positive influences on the brain 111
9. The eight noteworthy brain parts 114
What are neurons? 114
Synapses 116
Glial cells—the maintenance department 116
Neurotransmitters, electricity and chemicals 118
Cholesterol the smart maker 120
Blood, Oxygen and Water 121
Do we eat for our body or for our brain? 122
The myth that we only use 10 percent of our brain 124
10. Brain laws revealed 127
11. The law of intrinsic motivation 131
Our own intrinsic motivation 132
Triggering intrinsic motivation of other people 135
The first component is leading by asking 136
The second component is about money 136
The third component is about time value 137
The fourth component is about gamification 137
The fifth element is about positive group pressure 138
12. The law of self-determination 139
How to stimulate self-determination 140
The asking questions technique 141
How self-determination can lead to bankruptcy 143
13. The law of relevance 146
The skipping and swiping strategy 146
How to get noticed 148
Relevance of new learning methodologies 151
Improve your own internal relevance detection system 153

14. The law of communication 155
Why the brain distorts information 156
Guidelines for brain friendly communication 159
15. The law of healthy time balance 160
Subconscious frustration leads to sabotage 160
Healthy time balance formula 162
Guidelines to avoid subconscious frustration 164
16. Success management based on neuroscience 165
An untrustworthy brain 166
Error management 171
Success management 172
Brain laws necessary for every method 173
17. The brain knowledge vault 174
18. Never be the same 178
Learning and unlearning 180
19. How to apply in actual practice 182
Step 1. To recognize and research 184
Step 2. To acknowledge and accept 185
Step 3. To conclude and apply 186
20. Conclusion 189
21. Summary 196
22. Exercise Book: Why of Everything 198
How can we realize the start of our neural network change in
only 14 days? 198
A. Have you ever wondered? 201
B. Biological DNA related to passion 203
C. Brain school and brain knowledge 205
D. Our perceptive truth versus the fMRI scanner 207

E. Primitive natural resistance 209
F. The hormone factory 211
G. The triune brain theory of dr. Paul MacLean 212
H. A healthy brain 213
I. The eighth noteworthy brain parts 215
J. Brain laws revealed 216
K. The law of intrinsic motivation 218
L. The law of self determination 219
M. The law of relevance 220
N. The law of communication 221
O. The law of healthy time balance 222
P. Success management based on neuroscience 223
Q. The brain knowledge vault 225
R. Never be the same 227
S. How to apply in actual practice 228
23. SparkWise Quotes 230
24. Research and references combined 233

Foreword

One of our proofreaders wrote after reading this book: I am a critical person by profession. It is my job to 'not believe' what I see or hear. So the first time I went through this book, I was skeptical. As I am also skeptical towards personal development books, I did not know what to expect. However, after reading the book, all made sense—the build-up of the fundament, the logic behind all the information, your hypothesis and quotes. Using (neuro)science to support the reasoning, made more sense than I would have expected. How you guys explain the 'cause and effect' structure made me realize that I was only barely solving the 'effects' in my life.

The benefit to you as an individual is huge; whether you are developing as an individual in your private life, or as part of an organization, working with other individuals. The beauty of your book is that it is not about personal development, it is about personal disruption. In my opinion, this is the only way to let go of old habits and grow in the right direction. It might be an idea to offer this book with the 'red pill' and the 'blue pill' as in the Matrix, because once you have read this book: there is no turning back.

Your book is a revelation, helping to open the vault of knowledge all humans should have, to create emotional balance.

With emotional balance, it is so much easier to create and maintain your personal happiness. That happiness radiates towards others instantly. This is what I am experiencing right now, right here. Thank you so much for using me as a proofreader—it has changed my life in an astounding and positive way.

What to expect from this book?

What would you do if you discovered something so powerful that you had no choice but to share it with the world? We are opportunistic entrepreneurs, and not afraid to create challenges. We accept the challenge to be the ones looking outside the box. We believe it is possible to move from inside-the-box thinking, towards outside-the-box thinking.

At the same time, we are no scientists—nor do we want be. We do not have the time to devote 17 years to research, all to discover 1 millimeter of knowledge. Our clients, like always, need a solution yesterday. We love working with researchers/scientists; we love their passion and drive. Many of the scientists we collaborate with tell us that, due to the complexity of the human brain, they like to focus on specific or fragmented subjects to build more brain knowledge. Therefore, we are grateful to use all of their fragmented—sometimes still in research—information. We use their particular knowledge, and incorporate it into our own hypothesis—a very nice symbiosis. We challenge them to think outside the box; they challenge us to find proof of what we believe. We love working like that.

Taking the best from both worlds has helped us on our path to success, and given us the fortitude to maintain it over the years. Still, introducing a new view leaves the door open for people to disagree—with each other, and with us—and to shoot our vision and hypothesis down.

That is OK by us. This is what our book is all about: challenging each other, questioning uncompromising foundations and past beliefs. We get that our brains are not willing to change easily—excellent...:) Let's rock and roll!

When watching our current world, we see almost 7.5 billion people struggling. They struggle with many lifelong questions. Most of the time, they struggle with the same questions and issues, which are creating the same internal and external conflicts. Even when humans believe they are completely different, based on culture, race or skin color, they still act the same. So would it be fair to say all humans are the same in their way of acting and thinking? No? Well, are you ready to find out? We might surprise you with what new research has uncovered on this very topic.

On a global level, we find the same questions being asked, over and over again. Questions like: how was the Universe created—if it was created at all. How long have humanoids existed? Does God exist? Now some of those questions created beliefs and behaviors. These beliefs and behaviors have triggered many wars, poverty, and fear among millions, and created deeply entrenched hate, incomprehension, global issues, and a negative spiral that lasts centuries. Other major questions like, will there ever be peace on planet Earth? Will science cure our major health issues? Will we become hybrid humans soon? How can we manage the overpopulation of our planet? Will we live on Mars one day? And we can't forget the most common, personal 'bucket list' questions: how can I become richer, happier, or more powerful?

We wondered why generations upon generations create a system whereby they are primed to think in a fixed direction; the system of monkey-see, monkey-do behavior. Are we prepped, primed, and programmed already? Do we prime our children from the day they are born? Maybe even earlier, when they're still inside the womb? If so, how is that possible?

Have we become distant from our true selves, because social obligations have become the driving force in our lives? Have we forgotten how much fun it is to create new things, new ways of thinking, and to share these with our family and friends? Mobile devices affect us daily, and make it very hard to disengage from virtual reality.

We wrote this book because the vast majority of global citizens do not understand the intriguing difference between cause and effect. Many do not grasp where the cause of human behavior starts. From a professional point of view, the difference between cause and effect has impacted both of us hugely over the past four decades. When optimizing organizations and the people working there, our first focus is on the cause—never on the symptoms i.e. effects. This focus is infinitely helpful, but we humans haven't been shown how to do this until now. We need to go to brain school. Sadly, such a school does not exist, yet we still trust our brains to help us make the right decisions, every single day. The scariest part of all this is that, based on recent feedback from the newest fMRI scanners, combined software, and the EEG, we now understand we cannot completely trust our brains.

Herein lies our dilemma: how do we move forward when we cannot even trust our own brains? Let's ease into things with an explanation of general human behavior. This will give you a simple, "open," easy introduction to this book, and lay the foundations for what we're going to uncover together. As we move deeper into this book, we will emphasize how to use this knowledge in personal growth within a working environment. We will explain our vision. We have formed our point of view over the decades by advising decision makers, high school teachers, psychologists, NLP masters, coaches, trainers and public speakers.

We are blessed to still work, and learn, in corporate environments—environments with a huge concentration of thousands of different people in one virtual space, trying to work and live together every day.

But to go back to our opening line: we have discovered something powerful. We call it **Spark Wise**, i.e.: the "sparkling wisdom" existing in your head. You've got to be able to unlock and apply that wisdom, or you've got nothing but stored intelligence. Stored intelligence, when it comes to our lives, is useless.

We believe we have found the key to open that vault of Intelligence and Knowledge. Travel with us on this "out of the box thinking" journey, and learn our hypothesis and visions along the way. It is the most exciting journey you will ever take.

SparkWise Quote:
"Knowing and understanding the cause, is the essential key to changing the effects and becoming brilliant"

1. Have you ever wondered?

Brainer 1

Have you ever wondered how your brain functions? Have you ever questioned how you create feelings, and how you store them in your brain? How you process and initiate your behavior? Are you curious about the dynamics of your everyday behavior, or your mood swings? Are you ever surprised by your own thoughts, behavior or feelings, or surprised by other people's reactions? Have you ever wondered why you are wondering?

Humans have wondered for thousands of years. In the past, great philosophers like Plato, Aristotle and Socrates wondered. But these great philosophers didn't know about DNA, or microorganisms like genes, chromosomes, and neurotransmitters working within our brain cells.

The question is: are we really smarter today?

Why are we doing it wrong?

As shocking as this may sound to many of us, 95% of human emotion is ruled by the subconscious brain. Our subconscious mind uses a relatively unreliable data filing and recording system, and we—as humans—are battling for our rights, based on that unreliable archive system. Doesn't that seem peculiar to you? The most primitive, fear-motivated part of your brain is scanning for differences, rather than similarities—a logical, and biological, imperative to our survival. Our brain relies on this system to alert us to changes and variances, as a way of protecting us. This system kept us alive in dangerous environments, but it also creates the basis for misunderstandings, and most of the internal and external conflicts of our time.

Building blocks

By examining the human brain using an electroencephalogram (EEG) and functional Magnetic Resonance Imaging (fMRI) scanner in real time, we are learning, step-by-step, how the brain operates. Our brain produces big data, which we can read with software, store in databases, and compare with big data from combined neurolabs worldwide. This creates benchmark data, from which we can create specific data.

Neuroscientists are progressing in their research at incredible speed. What once took decades to uncover, can now be achieved regularly in just months.

SparkWise was born, many years ago, out of a need to figure out how the brain functions, through the study of the latest neuroscientific insights. We needed to get back to basics, and not from a psychological point of view.

We needed to get to the root, the cause of every decision, and the chief constituent of the human brain, so to speak. We wondered – would it be possible to create building blocks, to teach others about the workings of their own brain? And so, we pushed forward. We now call these building blocks 'brain laws'. By identifying and acknowledging brain laws, you will gain much more clarity and perception in the workings of the brain. Brain laws can help you to gain insight into how your brain creates internal conflicts and inconsistencies between the subconscious and conscious. Through Why of Everything, we can finally share this knowledge with you, and curious people like you, all across the globe.

We can explore why we so often say YES and end up doing NO. Why of Everything explains how the brain and body produce and activate certain hormones, and why. We can also examine the effect these hormones have on decision-making, behavior, moods, cooperation, intelligence, information storage, and how we process information. We can evaluate the influence our brains have over fatigue, overwork, burnout and so much more.

Biological DNA before you were born

Let's start with the basics of life: our biological DNA. In this book, we draw a distinction between biological and social DNA. We won't weigh you down with difficult scientific jargon, but it is essential for us to understand why biological DNA is so important. Every decision, biological change, feeling or behavior is made on micro levels. Understanding that these micro-biochemical processes result in behavior and feelings is crucial. No longer are these processes "just happening" to us, leaving us in total surprise. We will explain how DNA is made up, and what its function is.

It seems technical, but as we make our way through the upcoming section, 'Biological DNA,' you'll find a much stronger understanding of the ACGT building blocks.

World view up to 8 years old

We have around 7.5 billion humans on this planet, without permanent harmony between partners, families, cultures, religions, thoughts, understandings and behavior within the same species. Where our upbringing and social backgrounds differ, we humans tend to hold on to our upbringing, fostering the differences between us.

From a very young age, we humans use our upbringings as a basic guide to living life. Over time, we forget we are programmed this way. As individuals, we believe that our way is the only right way. Our childhood and education from a very early age will be our personal reference point for the rest of our lives.

So we see two major influences playing a key role in shaping who we will be, and how we will proceed with the rest of our lives. Let's call these two influences 'nature' and 'nurture'. DNA, of course, is our nature influence—the part we cannot influence or change through rational decisions. Everything we're going to learn as we journey through Why of Everything, is the 'nurture' influence. This is the part that we each have the power to change.

The main question is, are these two projected references— nature and nurture—objective, and are they even your personal references at all? How much influence do external factors have at an early and later stage in life? How much impact have they had on preserving or changing your personality?

Rules versus intrinsic motivation

Regulations and laws are created by society, to structure general human behavior. Even with regulations and laws, the human brain still creates its own laws. These laws, based on sudden hormonal impulses, create behavior that we often regret later on.

There is an intriguing difference between emotional behavior and rational behavior. Why is that? Although the same brain generates both emotions and logic, one is so much stronger than the other. Which one of these two is the stronger one? Is there a biological difference between emotion and intelligence? Does the brain use a certain sequence—does it have a game plan—in its decision-making? Does one part of the brain rule over the other parts? If so, can we influence those rules whenever we want to? Well, yes and no.

Depending on how much you understand of the operating of your own brain, you can influence many of the processes we're talking about. Pressing rules on people will not create the best results nowadays. At the heart of this realization is the fact that intrinsic motivation and self-determination are two very strong inner, emotional, drivers.

History has shown that self-determined humans can achieve incredible results, just by following their intrinsic motivation. We have created methods to activate both self-determination and intrinsic motivation, to help you unlock your own incredible potential.

The build of your personality

The human race is fantastic at creating, and continuing, conflicts. Once conflicts are created, both parties believe they have all the right in the world to fight for their beliefs; for their perceptive truths. In this conflict's state of mind, they will continue the battle, without searching for a solution. We have even been known to pull our children and grandchildren into our conflict, through their upbringing and education, letting them carry the burden of it long after we have died. If this influences a human at a young age, between 0 and 8 years, it becomes very hard to get it out of the brain system. Once they are caught in this conflict state of mind, they are more likely to convince, even force, others to follow their beliefs.

They will create a group of believers, becoming stronger and more convincing, more determined to make others accept and adopt their beliefs. It is how like-minded tribes emerge. Through this process, generations upon generations are driven to fight for something that stems from a single belief.

A single belief, which has created a conflict between two people, sometimes thousands of years ago. Insane? Illogical?

Yes. Insane and not illogical, it is. Nevertheless, it is also a standard biological process started by our brains. We will explain later how this works on a neurobiological level.

Brain laws and your professional mindset

The daily dynamics of change within our current society are an instant and major challenge for the human brain. Our brain will hold on to what it already knows and what it has learned in the past, and draws on this. The brain does not embrace change, because it likes standardization.

It functions best by using brain laws. The fundament for those brain laws are thick neural connections on a cellular level, developed before and after birth. This fundament contains trillions of existing neural networks.

By contrast, today's society is changing at a very rapid pace. Standards are changing on a daily basis. The digitalization of society has created rapid disruptions in human history, the likes of which have never been seen before. The strong influence of accelerating technology, and science developments are very good examples.

The neuroplasticity (ability to learn and unlearn) of our brain is huge, though. The natural discrepancies within it experience an interesting phenomenon. On the one side, the brain wants to learn, and it is almost permanently in the "I strive to create a better version of myself" mode. On the other side, with the current daily overload of information the brain is compelled to process, our brain becomes somewhat superficial.

Our brain desires new, relevant information. However, what is relevant to the brain is not always clear. Once the brain determines that the information is not "to the point," it deems the information irrelevant, and immediately tunes out.

By learning brain laws, it will become clear how and when the brain chooses to process information. We will show you how you can make use of these brain laws, and how to implement them in your everyday lifestyle. Understanding and applying brain laws can drive your professional and personal development exponentially.

Our intention with this book

It is our aim to reach as many people, on a global level, as possible with this book—to share the newest findings from DNA and epigenetic research, neuroscience, neuromarketing, neurobiology, neuropsychology and endocrinology. In Why of Everything, we have collated the findings generated by these combined sciences annually, and deciphered all the complexities into plain, simple English. We trust this book will help you to improve lives. Yours, and all those close and important to you.

With increasing "common sense" among readers, we are confident it will create an avalanche of questions, new insights, resistance, philosophies, recognition and fresh hypotheses.

Further, we are excited to open the vault of sparkling wisdom every brain already contains, to create substantial personal growth performance and professional success.

To our brain, growth on a personal or professional level is the same. In the simplest terms, human beings wish to be happy and successful.

SparkWise Quote:

"When we learn to understand how the brain operates, we can enhance the quality of all decisions"

2. Biological DNA

Brainer 2

Our Biological DNA is built up of 50% of our father's DNA and 50% of our mother's DNA. Our father and mother have that same build up from their parents, and their parent from their parents. Thus, chains of ancient DNA are transferred and passed down over many generations. Still, the DNA build up is always unique to each person. Even one-egged twins have an individual buildup of DNA. One twin will still have different DNA to the other. Our heritage is an important part of our personality and biology; one which we cannot influence through our intelligence.

Since DNA is completely capable of self-replication, both strands of a DNA molecule contain the information needed. Our DNA will replicate to make a full DNA copy with the same base sequence as the original molecule.

DNA is a (pre)programmed system, with the information we need to live and act. This makes it the only part of our personality that we cannot influence. A "gift" from the past, containing the ancestral information which makes us who we are today.

Ok, now this part is a bit technical but it will explain how the building blocks of DNA influence your personality. Bear with us—it will be worth it. These chemical building blocks are called nucleotides. These building blocks contain three parts: a sugar group, a phosphate group, and one of four types of nitrogenous bases. The nucleotides themselves contain four types of nitrogenous bases, which are: (A) adenine, (G) guanine, (C) cytosine and (T) thymine.

The combination between pairs is referred to as AGCT, or ATCGCT, or any alternative combination. Each individual has a unique sequence of these bases. The unique bases determine what biological instructions are in a strand of DNA. For example, if a DNA test shows that the sequence ATCGTT is found, it might determine blue eyes, while ATTCGCT could determine brown eyes. Every standalone combination of these four letters represents a specific result.

The interesting question is: what part of our behavior, feelings and thoughts are imprinted in our DNA after conception? Psychological science is researching Executive Functions (EFs), with a focus on behavioral genetics. Studies and lab tests show interesting developments and new discoveries as to the genetic influence on thoughts and behavior.

What parts of our behavior, feelings and thoughts are projected upon us by our parents, through their "nurturing" influence, and that of our education? What parts are learned, what beliefs are developed, at a later stage? And this doesn't even touch upon the other influentials: grandparents, friends, school, media, and social rules, which all have leverage over us in the long run.

You could say we have two separate subconscious sources. One is our preprogrammed DNA. The other is an autonomous system, subject to the diversity of influence and programming of our educators.

How is our "world image" formed when we are at a young age—between 0 - 8 years? Is our paradigm fixed? By paradigm, we mean the non-objective lens through which you see yourself, and the rest of the world. We might look at the world and ourselves through a lens that is not objective, due to our DNA and historical or educational "gifts."

So many questions to answer, right? Now let's try to answer them, by exploring the latest Biological DNA and neuroscientific insights, and sharing our philosophy, hypothesis, and life experiences.

SparkWise Quote:

"What is the truth? A mixture of DNA, childhood and further education by believing the truth of others?"

3. Brain school and brain knowledge

Brainer 3

Brain school

In the Western world, we generally go to nursery school from two to three years old, and later on to kindergarten. We learn how to play with other kids, how to behave in a group, and to listen to our teachers. We continue our education for the rest of our lives, learning interesting, and sometimes boring, topics.

At school, we learn a massive variety of subjects: economics, languages, algebra, math, history, geography, and biology—the all-important study of our organs. History shows that roughly 25% of what we learn at school is applied later, in our professional careers.

Something is missing. Unless you were into neuroscience as a kid, you were not taught one important aspect of yourself—how your brain operates. Because we do not have another brain alternative, we rely on our individual brain every day. Neuroscientists and technology have advanced the general understanding of the functioning and processing of our brain. This is an interesting development for some; a disruptive feeling for others.

Participants in our workshops and seminars often assert: "my brain made me who I am today and I am successful." You might be thinking the same thing, right now. We challenge participants in our workshops and seminars to engage in exercises. On average, it only takes a few exercises to assure everybody present that they cannot always rely on their own brain. The brain sometimes makes ridiculous, weird and unexpected decisions. It might be interesting to put trusting your brain to the test.

For example, look at the optical illusion by Samsem on the next page. Is it moving when you look at it and move your eyes? If so: can you still rely on your brain?

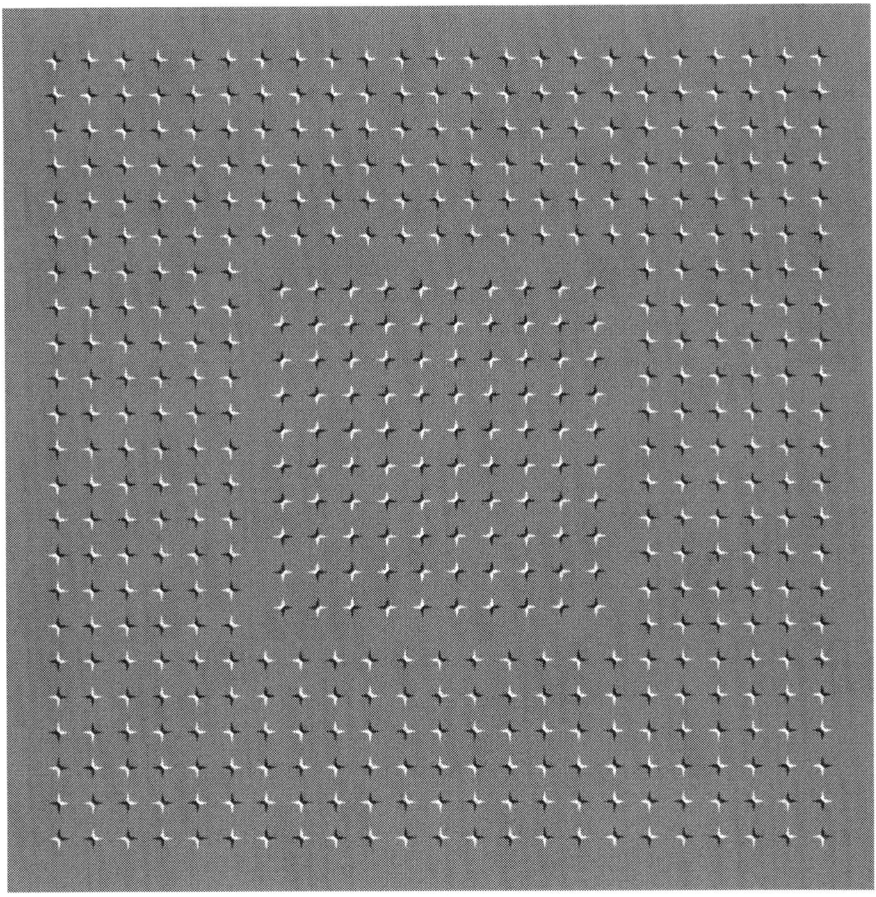

Although we cannot always rely on our brain, we can achieve good things in life. To become even more successful and emotionally balanced, we should question ourselves: if we could avoid most of our current mistakes, would we be more successful? Do we realize why we were successful in the past?

Has there been an element of sheer luck, which added to our success, or was it all premeditated? If we comprehend how to create success, would we be more effective in the future?

We have developed elements to create and duplicate success. With detailed knowledge of brain laws, it becomes easier to avoid historical, repetitive mistakes. From there, failure and success are like communicating vessels. When the chance of failure goes down, the chance of success goes up. Therefore, this new knowledge will obviate most of our daily mistakes. Some of you might have used the "learning by doing" technique, which was an acceptable way of learning in the past. Society was developing slower back then; as a result, there was enough time to learn by just acting.

This is not possible in today's knowledge driven society. In a knowledge driven society, all people have instant access to knowledge at the same time. The current generation is questioning their educators; why should I learn this now, when I could obtain it whenever I want to on my digital device? This means everybody has instant access to solutions, through the same knowledge source.

Through advances in technology, we are more aware than ever of the number of mistakes our brains are making. Some of those mistakes were learning opportunities, but most we would have rather avoided—especially those that harmed us emotionally.

If our educators had taught us how our brains operate, we could have identified the process our brain employs to make basic mistakes, long before now.

We need to learn, from an early age, how our brain operates. Right now, there is a massive lack of education for brain knowledge. Building and developing your brain knowledge changes your life in a way you cannot imagine.

So let us start the journey by inspecting our 'thinking process'. It's interesting to learn that the ratio—the intelligent part of the brain—provides for around 5% of the so-called 'intelligent' decisions we make daily. As we touched on earlier (because sometimes repetition helps the brain to better store information), this brings us to the staggering conclusion that over 95% of our primary decisions are initiated by the subconscious brain. The subconscious brain is seen as a less, or un-, intelligent brain section. It feels and acts, rather than thinks. Unfortunately, we have little to no control over this brain part.

As we dive deeper into this book, we refer to the subconscious and conscious most of the time. From our point of view, we find it important to establish the distinctive differences between these two brain functions. Because they have such complete differences in the registration and processing of information, they clash often. They tend to create internal conflicts, leading to internal stress, apart from external influences. Our subconscious determines our feelings, which in turn determines our direction of thinking, attitude, behavior and decisions. Often, our ratio is taken out of the decision-making process. That means that, essentially, we are taken out of the decision-making process. Our subconscious brain, being driven by DNA and an autonomous system, is determining our level of failure or success.

There is another element we need to feature. There is a specific difference between thinking *(conscious i.e. ratio)* and feeling *(subconscious i.e. emotions)*.

The subconscious brain manages how we "feel." We "feel" emotions; we feel happy, we feel angry, we feel uncertain, we feel suspicious, we feel sad. We communicate and respond to other people based upon the feelings we register.

The subconscious part, for example, establishes in a fraction of a second who we like or dislike. That determines with whom we will, and will not, work. Isn't that fascinating? We all strive for happiness and success, yet we cannot control the brain part that is responsible for achieving these goals. Is there a way to gain more control over our emotional decisions, and to carry out a certain amount of ongoing success? Yes. From our research and practical experience, through working with thousands of different people since the 1980's, we have discovered that there is.

Technology and neuroscience have come to the rescue. We now have a much better understanding of how the brain functions. That specific cooperation is a huge step for humankind. Now, we can look inside the active brain in real time. We can see how electricity between neurons is fired, how neurotransmitters carry their messages, and in which location of the brain the first, second and subsequent decisions are made.

Thanks to this breakthrough, we now know we cannot trust the first indications that our brain gives back. It has created a huge impact on our perception of our daily functioning, collaboration, registration, and belief of what is true and not.

This has influenced our way of understanding the human brain in a major way. This knowledge affects both the private and professional decisions we make. It therefore influences the general profit of an organization, and its future successes.

SparkWise Quote:
"Our protective fear system activates our natural resistance to any form of change"

Some people are convinced they are better than, more intelligent than, or even exalted above, others. We all know a few people that fit this description. It would surprise these people to learn that neuroscientists have discovered that the functional design of the brain is almost equal in everyone. It does not matter what skin color we have, or whether we are educated or not. It does not matter where we were born, or whether we are male or female. That makes us less unique, from a biological point of view, than we would like to believe. But there is an advantage here. When we understand how our own brain functions, we also understand the functioning of the brains of other humans.

When we understand the brains of others, we are in a much better position to use this knowledge to influence and treat each other in a positive way.

When we develop a deeper understanding of how the brain operates, we can influence the quality of a decision. We can put people in their emotional strength. Decrease people's insecurities and, additionally, the number of basic mistakes they make on a daily basis.

On a commercial level, we have discovered how to activate the intrinsic motivation of leaders and their coworkers. We can drive increased productivity and profitability, just to mention a few commercial possibilities. More than this, how does the knowledge of the function of our brain lead to a better total adjustment?

An organization, or a company, consists of divisions. A division consists of departments. Departments consist of teams, and teams consist of people. Therefore, organizations are people. The success or failure of an organization is created and defined by the people working there. People that communicate clearly work constructively, and are making wise, quality decisions.

This is not only important to our own success, but also to the success of an organization, and to the success of the society we live in. If our aim is to diminish conflicts: divorces, disputes, wars—we should send everyone to a brain school.

Through SparkWise, we are using a multitude of platforms to teach, explain and train people how the brain operates. We are educating businesses, groups and couples, university students, and people with no education at all. Everyone, every brain, can understand the information we share. Every brain is absorbing the valuable ingredients we bring to the table. This, to us, is very rewarding. Most participants respond: "If we had this brain knowledge years ago, we would have been more successful." Our mission, therefore, is to help people in achieving their goals.

Brain Knowledge

When we want to repair the engine of our car, we need to lift the hood and inspect what's inside. Even if we have no clue how the engine works, curiosity drives us to lift the hood when something goes wrong.

If we cannot fix the problem, we call an expert. The first thing an expert does is lift the hood, and examine the engine with his expert knowledge.

If we have a psychological or emotional problem, it is in our nature to try and solve it ourselves. If we cannot fix the problem, we might go to an expert—a psychologist, for example. We all know the cliché of a patient lying down on the psychologist's sofa. The psychologist, as an expert, asks many questions, and the patient explains their situation.

The big question here is: how can psychologists make a proper diagnosis, when they cannot see what is going on inside the brain during this process? How can they fix our engine without lifting the hood?

With the new technological and neuroscientific knowledge available, psychologists could benefit greatly if they could see what is going on inside the brain. Having access to, for example, a mini fMRI scanner and EEG, they could more readily form a proper diagnosis, in real time. We can conclude that a mechanic cannot fix an engine without lifting the hood and utilizing proper diagnostic tooling. The same applies for a psychologist.

Without looking inside the brain in real time, a psychologist is more likely to treat symptoms instead of the cause of a problem. Would it not be better to focus on the cause of the problem—a lack of knowledge of the functioning of the brain of the patient—instead of treating symptoms?

When we talk about symptoms, we are talking about emotional reactions, root behavior, and primary responses to a host of daily situations. Treating symptoms might help short term, or not at all. Treating symptoms does not address the cause of the problem.

By solving the cause of the problem, by being more educated in the functioning of our brain, we can create a better "us." This way, we become wiser, just by learning and understanding how our brain, one of our most important organs, is operating.

The logical starting point is to explain, in simple terms, how our brain is built, biologically speaking. What tissues and cells make up our brain? How do they function? And why are they so important, anyway?

Addressing these questions leads us to how they store information, and how they help us to make balanced decisions. They also open us up to what we need to do to ensure that our brain remains sound and healthy.

In the next few paragraphs, we will explain the basics of our vision. We have chosen, on purpose, to take some shortcuts. Some of the information is technical, but we will not dive too deep into all the explicit technicalities. We want to share this valuable information in an accessible, clear way.

Our brain is composed of a wide and complex variety of tissues and specific cells. We are only going to touch on eight noteworthy elements and their fixings, uses and functions.

The eight elements we are exploring here are neurons (brain cells), synapses, glial cells, neurotransmitters, cholesterol (fat), blood, oxygen and water.

In our seminars and training sessions, we regularly hear the assumption that men and women have quite different brains. That is not entirely true. But let's start with something fun— the basic differences between the male and female brain. Why does our behavior sometimes seem so strange to the opposite sex?

Differences between the male and female brain

The normal, healthy brain of an adult female weighs between 1000 -1200 grams, and the brain of an adult male between 1200 - 1400 grams. The male brain is 10% heavier than the female brain. The difference in weight does not imply that men, biologically, are more intelligent than women.

Although the "functional" design of the brain for the two sexes is the same, there are some noteworthy differences. One distinction is the Corpus Callosum. The Corpus Callosum is the bridge that connects the right and left hemisphere. This part in a woman's brain contains more neural connections and networks than in a male brain. Therefore, the bridge is a little thicker.

This is why it is widely believed that in a woman's brain, everything is connected to everything else. In our live workshops, we often ask the participants to give examples of daily differences between male and female brains.

Let's share one of our funniest examples:

"The whole family is gathering to watch a movie. Right before the movie starts, the wife says she has to go to the bathroom first. When she is passing by the kitchen, she feeds the cat and cleans the two dishes left in the sink. On her way to the bathroom she passes the washroom to put the laundry in the dryer, and then comes back, forgetting she wanted to go to the bathroom in the first place."

Now this might seem funny, but it is a story that so many couples can relate to.

A male brain works differently under the same circumstances. The male brain functions like a storage room full of containers. Each container holds specific single data. The data in one container is not connected to the data in another container. Therefore, when he has to go to the bathroom, he goes to the bathroom—that is his single focus—and then he comes back to watch the family movie.

Here's another example of single focus:

When a man has to go to the attic to get his drilling machine, he gets his drilling machine. His wife has put the laundry basket at the bottom of the stairs, on purpose. In her line of communicating, she's hinting to her husband to take the too-heavy laundry basket to the attic. However, his male brain doesn't pick up the hint to move the laundry basket sitting at the bottom of the stairs. The male brain, directed by testosterone, prefers to receive and execute specific tasks, much to the annoyance of his spouse. Most men do not understand why their spouse is so annoyed because in the male mind, the two independent single items (*laundry basket at bottom of the stairs* and *drilling machine*) do not connect in any way.

Another funny but practical example we often find in our sessions is:

When a woman asks her husband to take the garbage out, his first reply will be "ok honey, I will." The female brain means (hints) to put the garbage outside right now, so her brain expects the task to be done immediately. But the male brain might think "ok, I will do it" after watching football on TV, or finishing a beer, or finishing the game, or watching videos on YouTube, or the next morning when I leave to go to work, or when the garbage smells. To make sure that the man will do it now, his spouse needs to ask: "darling, will you be so kind as to take the garbage outside within the next 5 minutes?"

The main differences between male and female brains are hormones. The dominant male hormone is testosterone. One effect of testosterone is that men like to believe they can do almost anything, at any time. The effect of the testosterone hormone triggers over-self-confidence and, as a result, men take more risks.

For example: when a man drives a car, he is likely to take the bend in the road home faster and faster each time. Eventually, he's likely to take the curve too fast and, as a result, spin out. The male brain will conclude that it was not his fault. It was the car, the brakes, the road, the weather, the tires, the sand, or mud, or anything other than the man himself.

Testosterone is also responsible for sexuality, business drive, the focus and creation of success, aggression, dominance and fights. Historically this was handy, but not now that we have moved into the knowledge era. In the knowledge era, a brainpower driven society exceeds physical strength. Moreover, as men become older, testosterone levels diminish drastically. In turn, they become less aggressive, less sexually driven, and less active. Generally speaking, they become milder.

The dominant female hormones are estrogen and progesterone. One effect is that women, in general, have more of an eye for detail then men do. These hormones make them excellent micromanagers. Women are, as a rule of thumb, more risk averse and competitive, in a different way. Women rank each other based upon who they are as a person, and less upon what they possess, while men rank each other on what they possess; money, power, status, muscles, and will place less value on personal qualities.

It is important to realize that hormones have a major role in determining how we feel and act; how we communicate, and how we decide.

In our experience, we have found that the right mix of males and females in teams within companies outperform an all-male, or all-female team. A male/female team with mutual respect and equal intelligence performs around 25% better.

To capitalize on the capabilities and strengths of each gender, we should not concentrate on the differences between the two. We should learn to focus on how we can make use of the specific male and female capacities, in order to enhance commercial possibilities.

SparkWise Quote:
"Our well-equipped subconscious worked well in nature, but does not operate so well in today's concrete jungle"

4. Our perceptive truth versus the fMRI scanner

Brainer 4

What is the truth? Is there only one truth? Is it what you believe? Is what you believe created solely by you, or is it the mixture of DNA, childhood and further education, by believing others and the influence of general media? If two people study the same course at the same time, will they be able to learn and store precisely the same knowledge in their individual brains during that time span? No, they will not.

These were just a few of the questions we posed to neuroscientists, when we ran across the subject of "The Truth." As it turns out, "The Truth" has many parents.

Our educators build the basic foundation of your personal, and therefore perceptive, truth at a rather young age. Other educators like your parents, grandparents, school, culture, media, games, internet, religion, and, later in life, experiences, add to your perceptive truth. The truth will be altered over time in many respects—by anxiety, for instance. If a dog bites you at a young age, your perceptive truth will advise you that dogs are dangerous creatures. Therefore, it is impossible to accurately respond to these creatures for the rest of your life. The fear system in your brain will immediately respond when you see a dog, preparing you to either fight, or flee from the scene.

So, does the concept of truth exist? This is a rather interesting question. It is practically the same question as: does gravity exist? Well, does it? Based upon what we experience, we would say yes. When we drop something, it falls, right? Therefore, we can see and experience the effects. However, every truth or scientific fact was born as a single opinion about the unknown. Every truth, every fact, begun its life as a hypothesis. That single opinion gradually became a perceptive fact, as evidence piled up to support it.

Galileo was talking about gravity around 1600, but Isaac Newton is credited with discovering it sometime during the summer of 1665. "The Principia," where Newton first wrote of his findings, was published in July 1687, and we still work with his theory four hundred years later. Despite this basic theory holding strong for four centuries, new discoveries are calling it into question. Recent findings about dark matter, and dark energy thought being the largest substance in the universe, are raising new questions.

Dr. László Dobos, co-author of the "Monthly Notices of the Royal Astronomical Society" (March, 2017), and teacher at Eötvös Loránd University, contributes to this new school of thought.

Through his research team of Hungarian-American scientists, we are told: "We need to find new formulas to explain movements of stars and planets." We need to consider the traffic of future spacecraft through outer space, and even the acceleration of outer space, itself. This is thought-provoking stuff.

Albert Einstein is another interesting case. Although he was not a genuine mathematician, like Isaac Newton, Leonhard Euler, Carl Gauss, Carl Jacobi or David Hilbert, he has pushed our development forward significantly. A major part of his way of thinking was based upon mathematics.

The exciting puzzle here is: What if Einstein and the great mathematicians of our time are not entirely right? What if they're not right at all? What if another method of calculating, light years away from the standard mathematics that we understand now, emerges in the next 25 years? There could be a framework coming that we don't even know yet. Such drastic changes could stem from the random artificial intelligence created by a chain of smart computers. Or, a simple mistake in a laboratory could lead us to new insights.

As we are starting to see, the concept of truth is not a fixed statue. It is dependent on time, place, previous knowledge, and the willingness to undertake fresh, temporary theories and insights. Here is where the brain creates a dilemma.

Let's look at one of the major questions on planet Earth. Does God exist, or not? Both the religious person and the Atheist "believe" that they are right. Neither can evidence that they are right; even though their brains are willing to defend their beliefs until death do us part, so to speak.

In 2009, a very interesting study by Sam Harris, Jonas Kaplan, Ashley Curiel, Susan Bookheimer, Marco Lacoboni, and Mark Cohen was presented.

The study is called: 'The Neural Correlates of Religious and Nonreligious Belief.' This study shows intriguing insight into the religious and nonreligious brain. What it reveals to us is that the brain appears to be content-independent. It makes no distinction between the belief in God, and the belief that there is no God. With the use of the EEG and fMRI, both brains exhibit similar activity in 'the belief.'

Once our brain has accepted a truth that was created in the past, it is not willing to let that truth go. Thick neural connections are made over time. Our brain will use these neural connections constantly, as a highway of neurotransmitters, electricity and other cells. It will take a lot of physical energy to create new neural connections.

Your brain is energy efficient—it does not like to expend too much effort. It will use the existing working system to explain the why, how, and what, of everything. This system of natural biological resistance creates conflicts in our brain. It is driven by our automatic autonomous subconscious, and it is very fast. We can measure this with an fMRI scanner, because it measures Blood-Oxygen-Level-Dependent contrast (BOLD). So, BOLD contrast measures brain activity by detecting changes associated with blood flow.

An EEG measures the electrical activity of the brain. In conjunction with the fMRI scanner, you will get an impressive insight into what is happening inside your brain in real-time. If you're looking for an example of the latest technological developments, look no further than the Glass Brain. Developed by neuroscientist Adam Gazzaley and Philip Rosedale, the creator of Second Life, this is where neuroscience and technology meet.

The combination of the EEG and fMRI was the start of an exhilarating period of fast growing brain knowledge. New, more reliable, software was developed to register and process the big data produced by brain research using the fMRI. Laboratories and scientists all over the world started to work collectively. This gave humanity an innovative, important, and exciting insight into how the brain works. Almost 3 centuries down the road, we now understand, so much better, how the brain functions.

More than this, we better understand what kinds of hormones the brain activates under certain conditions. Science is an accumulation of hypotheses, scientific observations, complete mistakes, non-science, and out-of-the-box thinking from sometimes-narcissistic talents. Armed with this new knowledge, we can look back and refresh what scientists have claimed as their truths over decades. Science and technology are independently progressing in a disruptive way.

In today's open global society, we can see the same inventions and ideas are often created simultaneously, at different places around the world. Free access to information is the new way of working together. Continually learning and adapting to the new world is necessary to our survival. It's no longer a luxury. Facing this new demand, we have to contend with our brains' natural resistance to rapid changes. Now that we've learned that the brain likes stability and, in essence, hates change, how are we going to make our brains accept change as a necessary part of life?

Well, evolution helps. The neuroplasticity of the brain helps a great deal. Each new generation has another starting point of learning, based upon the latest technology and scientific developments. Therefore, if technology and science are moving faster than a human brain can follow in its lifetime, the backlog already exists.

The new generation has no trouble following it because it is their starting point. Cutting straight to the point, they do not know any better.

Their brains are already primed to travel in new directions, with less primitive resistance towards new developments. Their whole upbringing consists of diversity, and they are accustomed to the rapid changes we experience today.

The challenge lies, then, with adults. We have already chosen a certain path, belief, direction of development, education, or perceptive truth. The major challenge nowadays is to keep the brain flexible and open to new developments, rapid changes and increasing knowledge. In contrast to our past, the older generation is no longer the only mentor we've got. Their perceptive truths, the ideas they are holding on to, are fading rapidly. Age, education and knowledge are no longer enough to boost the new generation into a new time and era.

So why do older generations have difficulty with changes in general? How is their natural resistance activated when a change appears on the horizon?

SparkWise Quote:
"Subconscious determination often conflicts with rational thinking, while intelligence at the same time is certain it considered all possibilities"

5. Primitive natural resistance

Have you ever wondered why people do not carry out what we ask of them, even though they have said "Yes"? Have you ever wondered why people like the new plans, but do not follow up on them? Have you ever wondered why people wait until New Year to create resolutions, and pull the plug on them before mid-January? It is so common, that people have even pinpointed a date by which most of us have broken our new resolutions—"Blue Monday."

The brain sometimes acts in mysterious ways. People are sincere when they say "Yes." They mean it. But because of the way the most primitive part of our brain is configured, this answer is overruled most of the time. The bizarre thing is that what has become such a burden in modern times was once the part of our brain that helped us out-survive other species.

Fight, flight or freeze

In 1967, two sets of human bones were found near Kibish, Ethiopia. They were estimated to be 130,000 years old. Just a few years ago, a group of anthropologists, archaeologists and geologists were probing around Herto, Ethiopia, and discovered even older human bones. These bones are primary believed to be between 154,000 and 160,000 years old, but the latest computer technology stretched that date to 196,000 years old. Along with these bones, there was proof that these early humans used spears for hunting, and flutes for entertainment. Drawings in caves showed we had creativity, that we fabricated instruments and handled fire.

Over the years, more humanoid bones and skulls were dug up at different locations. This resulted in the registration of the Homo Erectus, the Neanderthal, Homo Sapiens, Homo Habilis, Homo Heidelbergensis, and Homo Denisova. Homo Sapiens survived the other humanoids, and matured into the humans we are today. Researchers came up with many speculations as to why we, the Homo Sapiens, could survive when the others could not. Most theories work on the basis that our faster evolution, and the improvement of our brain, played a pivotal role in the survival of our species.

Just recently, the National Academy of Science reported the finding of a humanlike skull, unearthed from the Aroeira cave site in Portugal. It is considered the oldest human cranium fossil ever found in Portugal. Through precision dating of the stalagmites and sediments surrounding it, the skull is believed to be 400,000 years old.

An essential ability of the human brain is to identify different levels of danger, instantly. There is one part of the brain that is responsible, and on the lookout, for danger. That part is the amygdala, and it works in close cooperation with the thalamus. The amygdala and thalamus are part of the Limbic system. In case of danger or a threat, the amygdala takes control, bypassing the intelligent part of our brain within milliseconds. This phenomenon is known as the "amygdala's hijack." It is here, when our amygdala hijacks the entire brain, that we do the things we tend to regret later. The amygdala is involved in, and responsible for, what we call the "instant non intelligent emotional response."

Brainer 5

The newest, largest, and most intelligent part of the brain is the cortex/neocortex. We use this part to communicate, to reason, to compare, and to solve problems. When in use, the cortex/neocortex produces and absorbs a large amount of energy. It uses much more energy than the subconscious brain. Another important fact is that the subconscious brain operates much faster than the cortex/neocortex. Current technology has calculated that the subconscious sector of the brain responds around one million times faster than the cortex/neocortex.

For our computer savvy readers, if we compared this to a computer, our subconscious operates at around 40 million bits per second (i.e. 5 MB per second), while the conscious part of the brain reacts at around 40 bits per second.

Within just 250 milliseconds, the subconscious brain determines whether a situation, object, or person, poses a threat. It does that based upon standardized reactions by the subconscious brain, which, as you now know, is passed on through our DNA. You might know it as "instinct," but it is a pre-programmed brain function, and it is not intelligent at all. It will react instantly, and drive us to one of three very limited outcomes: fight, flight or freeze. Even today, that part of our brain functions in the same manner.

Where does resistance come from

From this vantage point, the compelling question is: what does the amygdala see as a threat. In ancient times, it was obvious. Everything that could eat us, or was poisonous, was dangerous. When we saw something orange, with black stripes and long teeth, hidden in the bushes, the lifesaving protective system in our brain recognized that it was something which considered us to be food. It would make us run and hide as fast as we could, without taking time to consult the cortex/neocortex.

This system is profound. It is so well-honed that it recognizes all kinds of danger. It doesn't matter if we have never seen a large orange cat with black stripes before. Sadly, the great cats have become endangered species. We are no longer confronted with that kind of danger when walking the streets. Despite our relatively new urban jungle setting, our internal protective system still operates in the same way it did 400,000 years ago.

The issues most of us face in our daily lives are harmless: a new or unfamiliar situation, meeting someone for the first time, a change in direction, a person who disagrees with us or holds a different opinion. Arriving too late, missing a deadline, or not being able to do what we have promised to do.

Despite their tame nature, all these are registered as threats by our non-rational subconscious. Even your desk being moved without your input, to make room for a new coworker, might be considered a threat. As we can expect after what we've learned here so far, our non-intelligent brain will react in the standard programmed protective way: fight, flight or freeze.

The hidden behavioral constraints which rule our emotions

Every micro society—an organization, for example—has unwritten rules. We have dos and don'ts. The employees working within that organization may know the unwritten rules created over time. In that case, there is no written handout or rulebook. To find out what those unwritten rules are is an important task for any new employee in the first weeks of a new job.

New employees are tested by the existing employees and staff against those unwritten rules. The penalty for breaking these unspoken rules time after time is a lack of acceptance by the total group of coworkers. It can be severe and painful, and result in dismissal. This is a strange situation.

Human Resource departments have spent much effort, time, and money to find the right candidate. After several interviews, a psychological test, and tough salary negotiations, the new employee is hired.

Almost immediately, the new employee is turned over to the organization to be judged by invisible, unwritten, and unexplained rules.

As individuals, we are no different. We carry our own set of invisible, unwritten, and unexplained rules. But we take it a step further, selecting our friends and partners based upon our rules. When someone dares to cross our personal lines by breaking our rules, what happens? We get angry. We are insulted. Can you see what a strange and unfair system this is?

We are condemning others for crossing our invisible lines. How can we expect anyone to follow our rules, if we do not share and explain them first? This flawed system is the perfect playground for our most common conflicts. How can you expect a new employee to be successful without showing them the invisible, unwritten, and unexplained rules?

Clearly, this makes little sense to the intelligent part of our brain. The system we use is often the main reason people argue, fight, or resist, in times of change. Understanding how this ruling system works will help us to ask the right questions when we feel the anger rising. What unwritten rule did I cross? Have I explained this rule thoroughly enough? Another interesting personal question is: is this rule my own, or is it a rule passed down from my educators? Does this rule track all the way back to my ancestors, passed on by my DNA?

So while our rational brain realizes our error, our subconscious brain sees logic in this odd behavior. At least, this is the opinion of some scientists. It serves as a protection system. When someone cannot understand our unwritten rules, they do not match with us. They do not hold similar values, beliefs, rules and regulations. The conclusion we draw: they do not belong to our group of peers.

Allowing this person to enter our group might put the entire group in danger. This is the one thing our personal and collective protective system will not allow. In ancient times, when we lived in tribes, this protective system served us in valid, valuable ways. Nowadays, it is more like a handicap.

How does the brain process external information?

It is crucial to understand what happens when the brain receives external information. The ultra-fast subconscious brain filters the external information. It is important to know that our brain selects information based upon a few standard patterns. These standard patterns transform into brain laws. The standard patterns are:

1. Does this new knowledge or situation bring affliction or pleasure?
2. Is the new knowledge dangerous or not?
3. Does the new knowledge or situation conflict in any way with the perceptive truth already stored away in my brain?
4. Is the new knowledge relevant or not?

Based upon this process, which we explain in a very simplified way, our brain reaches a decision and a conclusion. When we are lucky, the subconscious part of our brain accepts the new knowledge, and it is passed on to the rational part of our brain. This will give us the opportunity to rationally explain why we have made that decision. It can take up to 7 seconds for the rational part of our brain to fabricate a convincing explanation.

Pain is 3 times stronger than happiness

Driven by our fear protective system, pain is three times more easily recognized than happiness. Our brain sees this as a legitimate process, protecting us and keeping us alive, but the consequences are tremendous. We already know that people continuously search for differences, as opposed to similarities, when they meet other humans for the first time. This system will rule commonalities out first, to make sure there is no danger. Once the brain has found differences, it will do everything to prove it is correct.

In this next paragraph, we'd like to share a compelling example of how our DNA-programmed subconscious forms decisions. It will decide, within a fraction of a second, if someone is competent or not.

In 2004, a study was conducted by Alexander Todorov, Anesu N. Mandisodza, Amir Goren and Crystal C. Hall on the ability of the brain to decide whether someone is competent or not based on just faces. The aim of the study was to prove, and show, that the subconscious brain part decides first, instead of the conscious brain part. They showed images of two elected politicians, for just half a second. Around 80% of the participants were correct in deciding who was, based on their initial reaction, the more competent of the two.

The bottom line is that we are NOT in any way objective. We all discriminate, in one way or another, even if rationally, we do not want to.

A meeting between two people is the smallest social group. In social psychology, this event is called a "dyad." In the timeframe of the dyad, both parties' brains are running through countless calculations, and answering countless silent questions. Is our relationship based on equality, or on an asymmetrical or hierarchical relationship?

What kind of body language am I picking up from this person? What kind of body language am I displaying? Is this family, friend, relative, or a total stranger? Is there emotional intensity, or distance? Does this person have potential as a mate, or not at all?

Whilst all this is going on in our brain, all we know is: *I like this person*, or *I don't like this person*. This explains the earlier emotional and subconscious-driven decision.

The entire dyad process is driven by our anxiety. Our protective system is kicking in. To overrule that watchful and fear-driven system, we can train our brain to search for instant similarities when meeting somebody for the first time.

The more specific the similarities, the more powerful the results. When the brain discovers shared similarities, the brain will produce dopamine, which is one of our happiness hormones. Dopamine makes the brain feel happy, less critical, more trusting of the other person, and in many cases—leads to the other person feeling this way about us. It is how relationships and friendships between strangers start.

Our brain has many separate registrations of pain. Insecurities, negativity, giving something of value away that belongs to us, these are all "pain to the brain."

How do you feel when the value of money is higher that the value of the goods received? When you pay more than something is worth?

In specific, when you make a cash payment. Paying by credit card, for example, is less pain for the brain because it moves the pain into the future. At this moment in time, the brain will not correlate paying with the credit card to instant pain.

This is why credit card companies have been so successful in the past.

A recent discovery caught our eye not long ago. It found that when we give someone a present, or do something for someone else, we value our effort three times higher than the receiver will register. Because we value our gift three times higher than the receiver does, our brain expects something in return, as an appreciation for the gift. Maybe not right away, but the expectation exists. Once we get something back, there is a high probability that we will perceive the present we receive at a lower value than the gift we gave.

Sometimes, we are disappointed—even frustrated, or angry. To avoid these negative emotions, therefore, it is important that when you give a present, you explain how important it is for you to give your present to that person. Sometimes it is important to explain how much trouble you have gone through to give that specific present.

SparkWise Quote:
"To give a present to someone is rated three times higher by the brain than receiving a present"

Earlier, we talked about the dyad. In that example, we said the smallest social group is comprised of two people. How is dyad behavior executed when more people are added to the equation? It may come as no surprise that the fear of being excluded from a group is also physical "pain to the brain."

It is difficult for our brain to act against the collective decisions of a group you belong to. Group pressure can make people act or speak in ways that directly contradict their beliefs. There have been several experiments to prove this behavior. You only have to type "social conformity prank" in your YouTube search bar, to find some hilarious examples.

Our favorite is a social conformity test done in the early 60's, with a group of people standing in an elevator. The group of people, unbeknownst to the candidate, is the research team. They are standing in the elevator facing the wall opposite the entrance. Shortly after, the candidate takes the same position. The total group shifts facing the left wall. The candidate observes, hesitates a little, and turns in the same direction.

Fear and negativity is contagious

So, we've learned that our brain produces, responds to, and runs on, hormones. One of these hormones is an important stress hormone called cortisol. In ancient times, cortisol was useful because we lived outside in a dangerous habitat. If we or a member of our tribe detected danger, the body would produce cortisol. Cortisol, interestingly, makes our muscles temporarily stronger. This was extremely important in a fight-or-flight situation, because superior strength could be the difference between life and death.

To make sure that the whole group reacts, we can actually smell the result of instant cortisol production. Doctor Li and his group of neuroscientists from the University of Wisconsin-Madison found the greater the stress, the larger the change in unpleasant smell. He published his study in the Journal of Neuroscience. When our nose detects cortisol from others, it is instantly triggered to produce cortisol as well. This switches the brain and body from standby to fight or flee. Immediately, we start to feel uncomfortable. It would not be a smart survival system if curiosity won over at that moment.

This biological system still applies now, as you might have experienced when going to a club. If you've found yourself in this setting, and two groups begin to argue, we start to feel unpleasant. We might say, "I feel a negative vibe in the club," or "the atmosphere is not right tonight, let's go somewhere else."

Cortisol levels can be measured in our saliva, skin, blood, and even hair. When someone with a high level of cortisol enters a room, we all produce cortisol to some degree. Within minutes, even seconds, we all would be affected by it. The result? Negativity rises, and people will make more mistakes. This is a key reason why people with a fundamentally negative world- or self-image are so dangerous to an organization. Not only do they frustrate others by their words or actions, but they negatively impact others by their higher cortisol level alone.

The subconscious rules over our intelligence

We human beings consider ourselves an intelligent species. We have a conscience, we can reason, we can talk, we can think steps ahead, we can plan, play games, create humor, be creative and so much more.

So we exist, right? We even think of ourselves as superior to other species—animals, fish, insects and even our own habitat: planet Earth. We have created a method to measure our intelligence, through the IQ test. With all the new findings in neuroscience, DNA, epigenetics and endocrinology, in close conjunction with the latest technology, is it possible that we are deluding ourselves? Are we as smart as we think we are?

As we now know, our brain produces and consumes a lot of energy all at once. Our conscious brain is using much more energy than our subconscious brain. If we were to ask you: what is 4 times 4, the answer instantly pops into your head. This is easy, because you learned your four times tables' way back at school.

Now, if we were to ask you: what is 215 times 1834; you can already feel how much time and energy it takes to come up with an answer. Most of our readers won't even try—although some will, just because they like a challenge. The majority of us will listen to the subconscious brain stating it is pointless to go through the exercise, due to its lack of relevance.

On average, we process between 50,000 and 60,000 thoughts and decisions, every single day. If we had to do this with our conscious brain, it would exhaust us before noon, and we would fall asleep. It would take far too much energy. Therefore, the brain has developed a set of rules in our subconscious to process most of our decisions. Our subconscious brain is faster, and uses a fraction of the energy the conscious brain does. The downside is that our subconscious is not very intelligent, and therefore we have no guarantee that it is making wise decisions on our behalf.

At this point, we come back to a brain quirk we looked at earlier: our subconscious brain does not always transfer the subconscious decisions to our conscious brain.

Over time, our subconscious brain has stored all kinds of registrations, feelings, experiences, and decisions, which are altered over time, as new information comes in. It is fair to say that our subconscious is making current decisions based upon a falsified archive system and a predominant set of rules.

However, our brain plays another trick on us. When our subconscious brain transfers its standalone decisions to our conscious brain, our conscious brain will create rational reasons to explain what the subconscious brain decided. Within this process, the conscious brain is convinced it has made a deliberate and intelligent decision. In reality, it has not. Most of the time, our subconscious is boss.

Let's look at an example:

Someone gets into a car accident, and ends up under water, inside the car. He cannot detach his seat belt. The conscious, intelligent part of his brain knows he needs to hold his breath. In less than a minute, the subconscious will notice that the oxygen levels are dropping in the brain and that in order to survive, he needs to breathe. Remember this part is not intelligent. It has no registration of being underwater and therefore, driven by the impulse to survive, he will take a deep breath. Although the intelligent brains "shouts" *do not breathe*, the subconscious will drive him to breathe anyway, and he will drown.

People that drown always have water inside their lungs, due to our protective non-intelligent survival system. Scary, when you think about it. Our brain makes hundreds of these subconscious decisions every day. It explains why humans make so many decisions that we are not aware of at all.

Primary resistance is located in the subconscious

Where is resistance found in the brain? What factors trigger a brain to resist? Can we reduce resistance? If so, how do we do that? In our coaching and mentoring sessions, many of these critical questions appear.

We meet resistance every day, both in our private and professional lives. Whether we aspire to work together towards a common goal, or we attempt to convince someone, or when we make an effort to sell something. The challenge here is that resistance resides in the subconscious brain. As you might recall by now, we are dealing with the non-intelligent part of the brain.

This part of the brain does not understand words, logic, facts, figures or statistics. When we experience conflict with someone, we will attempt to justify our "I am right" through words, facts and arguments. Here's the bad news: from a brain response point of view, that is useless. The harder we push forward and strive to convince someone how right we are, the stronger the resistance will become. As you've seen throughout this book so far, the subconscious wins most of the time.

This makes it challenging to manage a company or division without conflicts. When push comes to shove, we commonly resort to playing hardball. "I am the supervisor, and you need to do as I say," is a go-to response for so many of us. How is our employee supposed to react to this?

The intelligent part of the brain recognizes that it is smart to say "yes," and it convinces the sender that this is the right move. At the same time, the subconscious part of the brain says "no," frustrated by the fact it is being forced into going against its own will. This part of the brain will search for ways to sabotage the intelligent decision.

From your personal experience, you know your brain will sabotage. But because the subconscious part of the brain lacks intelligence, it cannot oversee the consequences of its actions.

This process generates an immediate internal friction between conscious and subconscious. The brain will register stress, and will set all systems to fight or flee. There are ways to compensate for the primary resistance, using a brain-friendly method. In the chapter 'Brain Laws,' we will explore these brain-friendly methods, and provide you with specific techniques that you can implement in every area of your life.

The urban jungle and stress

Our non-intelligent fear system operates in similarly to how it did 400,000 years ago. When our subconscious brain detects danger, we produce a bunch of stress hormones. Now, though, the danger has shifted from savage animals to the contemporary threats of the "urban jungle." We've explored some of the tiny changes that our brain might view as a threat—the new colleague, for example. We've talked about cortisol, produced in times of stress, and how it helps us fight or flee.

In nature, we would fight or flee and absorb the cortisol. In the urban jungle, we do not fight or run away when encountering stress. Because we're not using the cortisol hormones, they stay in our bodies for much longer. This is an unhealthy situation. When cortisol remains in our system, it destroys a lot of biochemical processes in our body, and even in our brain. Put simply, we need to get these cortisol levels down as quickly as possible.

In order to do this, it is important to understand how these hormones operate. We can learn how to diminish the cortisol levels in the brain and body when detecting stress. Cortisol production can become chronic, and higher levels of cortisol can become addictive. Worse still, when cortisol levels remain high within the body, it can lead to weight gain, depression, and hypertension.

High cortisol levels and chronic stress create burnout. When we spend too much of our time on activities our subconscious brain does not like, or does not want to do, it will manifest as continuous stress. This will create a continual production of high volumes of cortisol. When this continues over a longer period, we burn out.

A burnout is a deliberate subconscious decision. Our subconscious brain is warning us that we are on the wrong track. As we continue to push down this track, our brain punishes us for not being attentive to the subconscious brain.

What is the effect of cortisol on our daily decisions

What effect do high stress levels have on our daily decisions? The short answer is: stress hormones can have a positive effect. Stress hormones focus us on the assignments at hand. The hormones activate energy to perform for long hours, to meet deadlines, and to finish the job. We all appreciate that drive. Running on stress hormones, occasionally, is not a bad quality at all.

The extended production of stress hormones comes with a severe downside. We do not like to work in an environment where the people in charge are unreasonable; where a management style is authoritarian; where deadlines are unachievable; where we do not like our colleagues. In such a context, the stress effect is different.

The short-term effect is that we become ill more often. It always begins with little disturbances. In this state, we get a cold or the flu. Most of us can attest to the effect stress has on our quality of sleep. Eventually, we become run down, pale, and sallow. The body can create many low grade inflammations. These, in turn, affect the general immune system, and damage all sorts of biological processes in the brain and body. We exhibit behavioral changes. Often, people in this state deliberately frustrate company processes.

Higher cortisol levels also make it much harder to think. We make increasingly poor decisions, resulting in more mistakes. Remember how we discussed the way humans spread cortisol production to those around them? People will infect each other at the "stress department," and establish a negative in-company spiral. More subconsciously created mistakes are made. Stress is costing companies an awful lot of money and staff.

6. The hormone factory

Your endocrine system is a collection of glands that direct hormones towards different target organs. The endocrine system helps control all sorts of hormonal processes and systems, much in the same way that homeostasis controls the internal balance of our bodies' systems. Our brain plays a very significant role, too.

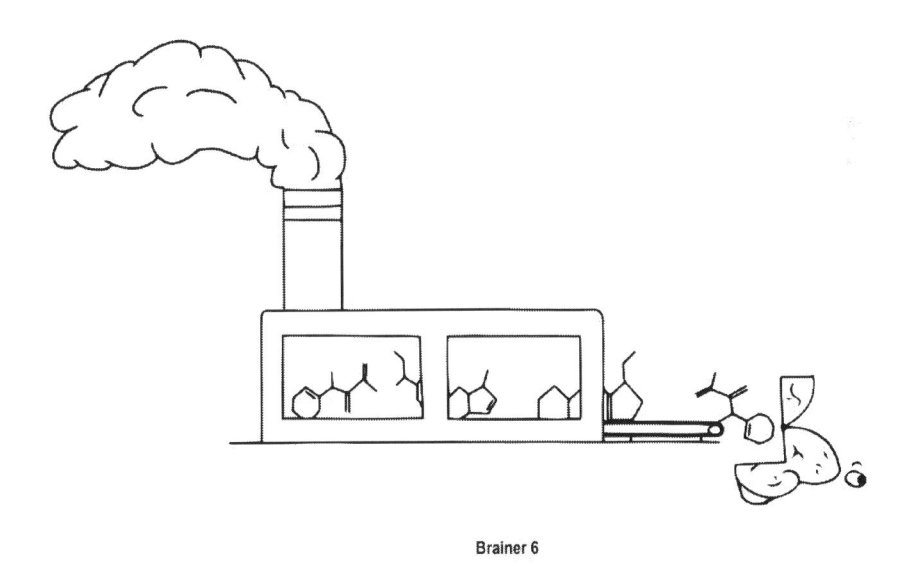

Brainer 6

Hormones are, in fact, a collective name for different groups: Amino Acids, Eicosanoid, Steroids and Peptides. But let's not dive too deep into the Latin names.

To make a long story short(er), some of the Steroids and hormones determine how we feel, what we do, and how we decide. This is why you make different decisions when you are happy than you would if you were angry.

Our emotional 'mood' has a strong impact on how we function, and so it is crucial to our failure or success. The striking fact is that we can, to a certain extent, activate our own hormone production. Even more amazing is the fact that we can activate or influence the hormone production of others.

That sounds weird, we know. But to some degree, we are already doing it every day. Think about how persistent you can be, how unwilling to give in when you argue with someone. Have you ever held your position on purpose, just to prove that you're right? By refusing to back down, even when you realize you might not be right at all, you are already steering the hormonal production of your opponent. Your opponent becomes as tenacious as you are, producing the same hormones as you do—and a mutual conflict is born. This mutual activation process only takes seconds.

When we learn to activate the appropriate hormones, we will have a great influence on our personal emotional setting, and that of others. Frankly, we become better verbal and nonverbal communicators. This will help to improve the overall performance of our coworkers. It will help to build stronger relationships with our partners and children. We can encourage others to do what we want them to do, without manipulating them. We can even motivate people to like and accept us for who we are.

So far, scientists have identified many different steroids and hormones. For the purposes of this book, we'll need to explore the three most prominent stress hormones. Each one has a unique task and effect. The hormones we'll look at are: Epinephrine, also known as Adrenaline; Norepinephrine, also known as Noradrenalin; And, of course, our old friend Cortisol.

We produce these hormones in demanding situations. Their functions play a major role in activating our brainstem. They also activate the registration of, and response to, anxiety, leading to a change in attitude.

Stress hormones creating negativity

Adrenaline

Adrenaline is part of our survival mechanism. It makes the heart beat faster and blood pressure rise. As a result, more oxygen is present in our blood and muscles, enabling us to respond quicker to threats. Adrenaline is released during fight and flight conditions—when we are under stress, under pressure at work, in pain, scared, or angry. Also, with extreme temperature changes, hunger, thirst, and physical pain, the body produces adrenaline.

Noradrenalin

Noradrenalin is a stress hormone and neurotransmitter, produced by the adrenal medulla and neurons (nuclei). It helps to focus and maintain oversight, so we can better handle hectic moments. It also masters stressful situations. Noradrenalin raises blood pressure, which stimulates us to be more alert, and to see the situation around us more clearly. Noradrenalin has a higher impact on emotions than adrenaline. Someone with a high level of noradrenalin can experience panic and anxiety attacks, and becomes tense or upset more quickly.

Cortisol

Cortisol prepares the body for fight or flight. It strengthens our muscles. It causes paranoia, nervousness, selfishness and alertness. As we saw earlier, this chemical can be contagious, and when produced continuously it will become dangerous. Cortisol is considered the general stress hormone. Every form of stress, in both physical and psychological states, releases cortisol. Cortisol reduces empathy and kindness, and it restricts the production of oxytocin.

When someone holds high levels of cortisol for too long, this person will become ill. Researchers are examining what cortisol does to heart and vascular diseases, cancer, type 2 diabetes, low-grade infections in the body, and destruction of brain cells (neurons). Because the brain does not separate fiction from reality, we can even trigger cortisol production just by thinking about a stressful situation. If, for example, we are describing a negative or traumatic experience that took place years ago, we will grow angry, frustrated or depressed again. Our brain doesn't draw the distinction that the situation is no longer a threat to us. This is why focusing on negative thoughts like regret, shame, debt, revenge, or constant worrying are so harmful. They all have an instant effect.

Hormones that produce happy or positive feelings

We carry four major positive hormones. Endorphins, dopamine, serotonins and oxytocins (EDSO). These chemicals play an important role in reward, joy, helpfulness, laughter, happiness and solidarity. We can produce endorphins and dopamine ourselves, whereas external influences—people, or our environment—spark the production of serotonin and oxytocin.

Endorphins

Endorphins involve the reward system of the brain. The central nervous system and the pituitary gland produce endorphins. We produce this chemical, for example, when we smile, or animate ourselves to carry out a special or bold task. Endorphins make us feel happy, even euphoric. Endorphins make us perceive problems as being smaller, and can eliminate pain as effectively as a dose of morphine. Thanks to endorphins, we are more inclined to make a positive decision in our subconscious. Now we realize why it is so important to make someone laugh. The release of endorphins, known as a "runner's high," eliminates pain and make us feel happy.

Dopamine

Dopamine plays a major role in decision-making processes, and contributes to feelings of joy and prosperity. We produce dopamine when we take action that, according to our brain, deserves reward. Dopamine is released, for instance, when we finish an assignment, reach a goal, or complete an item on a to-do list. Fine food, alcohol, and drugs are a reward, and therefore activate the release of his hormone. Dopamine is a behavior stimulant—the happy feeling we experience drives us to repeat the behaviors. It encourages people to plan and complete a task, and accomplish deadlines. It gives focus on visualizing goals. This is why a daily reward, or compliment, is so effective.

An immediate reward scores much higher for the brain than a reward in the distant future. Knowing short-term rewards score higher, how can we modify the way we manage staff? When we know that the brain values instant reward, we can recognize that monthly and yearly targets, and bonuses at the end of the year, do not serve us well.

To give a compliment when the tasks are completed is more valued by the brain's reward structure.

The disadvantage, and greatest risk, of dopamine is that it is addictive. It fades norms and values. We have all seen cases of this in the corporate world. Bankers, for example, who could earn massive financial bonuses, went for the premiums. Their moral standards vanished, and short-term profit became more important than long-term durability or responsibilities.

Serotonin

Serotonin has a positive influence on our memory. We release serotonin when we register pride, dignity, public recognition and gratitude. It creates a sense of self-confidence. We produce the most serotonin two hours after dawn. To produce and release serotonin, we need to have enough energy; therefore, a good, healthy breakfast is vital. Without the appropriate nutrients, the body cannot produce serotonin.

Vitamins and minerals increase serotonin production. We also release serotonin when someone we feel a connection to is complemented, rewarded, praised or honored. That could be a manager we like, a close team member or teacher we respect, or a member of our peer group. This is why programs like 'Employee of the Month' are so successful all over the globe, and why it is so important for managers to compliment and acknowledge others in their speeches. It boosts the morale of the group, and of the company. Serotonin makes people want to work for the group they belong to.

Oxytocin

Oxytocin is known as the "cuddle drug." We produce oxytocin by physical contact with somebody we like. A hug, touch or handshake is enough to activate oxytocin production. A high level of oxytocin fosters trust, security and solidarity.

This is one reason it's so important to shake hands, and to hold the grasp for at least two or three seconds. If you're not already doing this, try it; with people you meet for the first time, and especially when you come to a mutual agreement or deal. Without that degree of trust, it is difficult to arrive at an agreement. Oxytocin also reduces cortisol levels, and therefore stress. Recent research shows that it also impacts susceptibility to addiction, and improves health. Oxytocin builds up gradually.

We also produce oxytocin when we observe someone undertake an unselfishness deed, or be generous. A quick tip for supervisors and managers: sending an e-mail does not generate oxytocin. Taking time to walk by and give personal attention while talking does.

When we focus on our attitude, and its ability to produce one or more of these four chemicals within others, we are changing our micro surroundings. We are changing the world around us.

These chemicals stimulate us to do things ourselves, which flows on to our organization, our division, or our team. Employees, prospects, and clients, with a low level of EDSO will never become an ambassador of the company or brand.

All of these chemicals determine how we feel and behave. Because our brain does not distinguish between fiction and reality very well, we can actively influence how we, and others, feel. When we master this, we have an immediate impact on how coworkers will experience working with us.

The short and long-term benefits are a steady decline in failures on an individual level, and the creation of personal and professional success.

7. The triune brain theory of Dr. Paul MacLean

Brainer 7

Paul D. MacLean was an American physician and neuroscientist who, in 1960, founded the hypothesis that we have three brains, instead of one. He published many books over the years. One of his basic arguments was that the brain does not start as blank pages to be filled up. MacLean's work was a serious attempt to explain the basic functioning of the brain. His theory helped to develop a better understanding of the workings of the human brain. We know now that his concept surrounding brain activity was incorrect, but it remains a useful basic theory of how the brain operates.

Above all, it is easy to understand for us everyday people. His model illustrates, in a simplistic way, the complexity and behavior of our brain, and it serves the purposes of our book. Paul MacLean stated that we, as human beings, have three "different" brain systems with specific functions.

The three brains do not interact well. Paul MacLean's vision explains why humans so often make bad decisions. He also provides us a basic guide in how to become more successful.

The next few paragraphs will equip us with essential information: how those three different parts are operating, and how this basic knowledge will benefit us today. The first part is the so-called **brain stem** or **reptilian complex**, the second part is the **limbic system** or **mammalian brain,** and the third and final part is the **cortex/neocortex**.

Our brain stem or reptilian complex

Right at the top of our spine is the brain stem or reptilian complex—one of the oldest parts of our brain. This part functions more or less like an impulse system, which holds no intelligence or emotions. We share this with other species, like the hungry crocodile mother who will, without any emotion, eat her offspring to survive when there is no alternative food source. The main purpose of the brainstem is to regulate autonomous functions, like our heartbeat, respiration and body temperature.

Very few people can influence this portion of the brain. Those who practice certain forms of meditation for years, like the fakir, may have a higher chance than the rest of us. A well-known example is Wim Hof, internationally known as "The Iceman." Wim Hof can regulate his body temperature, maintaining it at 37 degrees, even when lying in a bath of ice cubes for 1 hour and 53 minutes.

By all (scientific) standards, he is an extraordinary human. Wim holds 21 Guinness World records, yet says, "What I can do, anyone can do. It is just having the right mentality, persistence, passion and knowledge of the working of the brain and central nervous system. That's it... and, of course, practicing every day." Wim calls it activating the inner fire.

Our fear system protects us. It is cooperation between the limbic system and the brain stem. The limbic system detects danger. When it detects danger, fear or pain, it activates the brain stem immediately. The brainstem will speed up our heartbeat and respiration. Our fear protection system handles our survival in dangerous situations. In that respect, we consider fear as a positive property.

Let's think back to the car accident example. This is a cruel, but very real, example of the clash between the intelligent and the non-intelligent brain parts, whereby the non-intelligent brain wins. In normal day-to-day life, the non-intelligent part of the brain wins many times. In turn, this leads to non-intelligent decisions.

But what are the implications of our non-intelligent brain ruling our daily lives? We know this section of the brain is dominant, and responsive to fear. What does this part of the brain classify as fear? Insecurity, the unknown, change, an opposing opinion, or a new colleague are all fear triggers, or "pain to the brain."

Let's look at some other situations that the non-intelligent section of the brain is putting in the "fear" category. Targets or goals that are out of reach, market disruptions, public presentations, a performance evaluation, walking towards— or talking to—the girl or man of your dreams. Add to this the perceptive references created in your brain's archive system from ages zero to eight years, and the biological DNA inherited from your parents and ancestors, and you've got a very extensive list of pain to your brain.

When the brain detects "fear," it releases stress hormones like adrenaline, noradrenalin, and cortisol, to activate all systems to fight or flee. When we release these hormones, some of our brain and body functions are put on hold. Digestion, hair and nail growth will stop.

The body needs all its energy to fight or flee. From a survival standpoint: so far, so good. Not so for the brain. Under this kind of duress, we do not access certain parts of our memory and intelligence. What this means for us is, it is very difficult to recall and process words.

Have you ever given a speech to a large audience? So many people are incredibly stressed leading up to delivering a speech. Many can't even recall their opening line. The more we fear forgetting our speech, the higher the chance we cannot reproduce it.

The same thing happens when we try to process the words spoken to us. That is why we are advised to bring a second person, when we go to a physician for test results. In that stressful situation, people will respond later, "I cannot even remember what the doctor said; I was in shock." It is not that we do not want to listen. The brain simply disables this functionality.

We can apply this updated information to so many situations. For instance, when people disagree with each other, they might shout, "you do not listen; I will explain it to you one more time." When the other person is in stress mode, it doesn't matter what you say—he/she will not process and remember it the right way.

Can you recall a time when you had an emotionally driven argument with someone who didn't share your opinion? We all have these experiences. It doesn't matter what we say, we can't convince them to agree with us. Now we know some of the reasons why. But what can we do to realize successful communication?

In our business, we train management to recognize the four stages of conflict creation. We teach them how to preside over a meeting in a brain-friendly, efficient, effective way.

Team members often disagree with each other in meetings. Human brains follow standard patterns. Therefore, it is not difficult to predict the course of a discussion. We have identified four stages:

Stage one.
If people disagree, they will repeat their arguments a few times to convince the other person.

Stage two.
When this does not do the trick, which is obvious with the knowledge we have now, they will use "power arguments" in the next phase. Their tone of voice becomes higher and louder. They apply phrases like "you don't understand me," "you don't listen," and "you repeat yourself." "I'm so fed up with you," "you are not convincing me at all," are some other (mild) samples of what they might say. At this stage, the meeting is being derailed from any intelligent course.

Stage three.
When the chairman does not intervene, the discussion will move on to the third phase. In the third phase, the participants will use even stronger words, and will try to hurt, and damage, each other. The opposition is profound and growing to its maximum level. The resistant behavior is escalating even further. In phases two and three, the non-intelligent section of the brain has taken over from the intelligent section.

Stage four.
Even when both parties recognize the symptoms, they still find it hard to react in a different way. In this situation, the subconscious brain has become boss. The non-intelligent subconscious will take non-intelligent action, like physical fighting, to win the debate. This is counterproductive, not smart, and leads to bad results. Results that we usually come to regret.

By learning to identify these four stages, we can use specific techniques to intervene and calm the subconscious brain down. With these techniques, we can steer the discussion in the right direction from stage one. The essence is to appeal to the limbic system in the right way. The limbic system is rather capable, and willing to learn and unlearn.

The Limbic system

In this book, we're going to put the limbic system in close alliance with the brainstem, as the two most important parts of the subconscious brain. It is significantly more complex than that, due to the left and right hemispheres' important roles, but we want to help you build the basic understanding you need to get the most out of what we are learning here.

The limbic system, commonly referred to as the mammalian brain, is located between the brainstem, cerebellum and cortex/neocortex. It consists of different sections. The amygdala, thalamus, hippocampus, limbic cortex and hypothalamus are the most well-known by people learning about the brain.

The limbic system is, in light of what we wish to write about in our book, important for a few reasons. One significant aspect is how it joins with both the brainstem and the cortex/neocortex. Because of these connections, the limbic system can somewhat calm the brainstem, and influence the cortex/neocortex.

To illustrate, we can explore the limbic system's influence in an everyday setting.

Humans are sensitive to their first names. This is referred to as "the cocktail party effect." When we are in a room full of people and someone calls our first name, we hear and respond. The amygdala, which is part of the limbic system, handles this reaction. Faster than we realize, it is establishing what has the potential to bring us pleasure or pain, and what is dangerous or safe. It filters what is relevant or irrelevant from the huge flow of information being received and processed.

Our first name is very relevant to our brain. It is part of our identity, created by our parents and other educators from the time we are born. We have been influenced by our name during our childhood. Parents and other educators have been calling our name on many different occasions, so our first name carries a high priority in our brain. Over the years, our first name has been registered in hundreds or thousands of different locations (neural networks) in our brain. Our brain will recall our first name as being very important.

When someone speaks our first name, the limbic system is sensitive and aware of what is happening. It needs to estimate whether the situation is dangerous or not.

When our name is called, the limbic system influences the brainstem into a "wait and see" position, to evaluate the situation. Even with a fear-driven active brain stem, calling our first name has an instant effect. When someone's first name is mentioned, the brainstem's fear mode is, at least for a fraction of a second, put on hold. Within this fraction of a second, we can activate the cortex/neocortex, and move an emotional discussion from emotion to intelligence.

Over the years we have experimented with the following technique and strategy.

In a heated discussion, someone's brain position will shift from the intelligent brain part to the non-intelligent brain part. The level of resistance at this point has increased, and `normal` conversations will have less effect.

To bring someone out of that emotional status, create a small pause. Look the other person in the eye. Then, use his or her **first name** in a soft tone. Next, ask a question relevant to the discussion you were having. Choose the question yourself, and offer up two possible answers.

For example: Joanne, by what you just said, do you mean…

1. a-b-c,

Or do you mean,

2. x-y-z?

What will happen is that the brain, not capable of multitasking, will switch to the intelligent brain part to solve the question, and choose between the two potential answers you brought to the table. The brain cannot be angry and work out an intelligent question at the same time. To sweeten the deal, so to speak, the brain likes to decide between two options.

Once Joanne has answered your question, you can take it a step further. Let's say Joanne chose option 2.

Continue with: OK, I think I understand. Just to be sure, do you suggest that by option 2...

1. d-e-f

Or

2. k-l-m?

You are giving Joanne another two options, within her chosen option 2. Now the brain needs to think a level deeper into the intelligent part of the brain, and will conclude that maybe its anger was misplaced—maybe this was a misunderstanding. You can continue this process two or three times, repeating until both parties have the same interpretation of what was revealed or discussed. With this technique, apologies come much easier.

Steering hormonal influences, as we do with this example, show how simple techniques drive the limbic system to influence the cortex/neocortex's thought processes.

In summary: slight pause, eye contact, use their first name with soft voice, question with two answer options, and repeat the process two or three times until the anger diminishes. We call this making use of the "Natural Relevance Detection" (NRD) of the limbic brain part.

By natural behavior, the NRD is active often. Here is a nice NRD example we all recognize.

Suppose you're in the market to buy another car. You are looking for a specific model (A) in a specific color (red).

First, we check online to see what kind of offers are out there. We watch videos on YouTube, read owners' experiences and reviews, go to the car dealer to take a test drive, and become even more enthusiastic after the test drive.

While driving home in our old car, we notice more red model A cars on the road than ever. In reality, there are no more or less of those cars, in that color, on the road.

Nevertheless, to our "NRD" brain part, the red model A car has become much more relevant. In response, it draws our attention every time it recognizes this new, relevant object.

NRD also plays an important role in learning and unlearning. Technically, at a cellular level, the design of our brain must learn something new or have an available alternative before it can unlearn an earlier opinion, habit or thought. Many people say: "I want you to stop doing that" because they are convinced that advice, tips and tricks work fine, to experience it doesn't have the impact they anticipated. The brain can learn new information fast. Remarkably, most people find it challenging to accept and learn another opinion or fact.

We will explain more about how this learning and unlearning process operates on a cellular level in the chapter "Never be the same."

Another interesting aspect of the Limbic system is its sensitivity for gamification. Allan Reiss and his coworkers at Stanford University performed brain scanning on subjects playing a simple video game. They measured gender differences in the mesocorticolimbic system during computer game-play. While gaming, the release of dopamine was high.

Most healthy people are highly receptive to Dopamine. This explains why around 75% of people of all ages enjoy gaming or games. Games are a very important tool for learning and change management. When applied the right way, gamification can be an important means of lowering natural resistance towards change.

Using gamification makes it much easier for people to accept change, learn a new situation, a new behavior, or a smarter execution. Our brain is fooled quickly and easily. Using that aspect with gamification can be a great way to drive people's learning.

For our protective fear system, playing a game is not as threatening as a real life situation would be. In a game, we can practice a new situation or desired behavior over and over again, without getting the full-blown standard fear reaction. That is a tremendous plus. The next big plus is that playing a game, and becoming better at it, also affects the reward system. Everything good comes in threes.

While playing a game, the brain creates new neural connections and networks. Every time we learn something new and relevant, our brain makes new neural connections. During that process, the brain lets go of old habits or behaviors, and accepts new, more relevant ones.

How can we use gamification to improve communication in sales? When we buy goods, our brain evaluates in three rounds:

Round one
The emotional decision to like, and want, the goods.

Round two
Our ratio produces rational motivations for wanting, and buying, the goods.

Round three
The ratio will calculate the value of the goods, to execute the financial transaction.

To increase sales, we need to know where the emotional buying system lives. We need to capitalize on this key round of the decision-making process.

The buying button is located in the limbic system

The human brain has a sort of buying button, and it's most commonly known as the "impulse buying system." The buying button lives in the limbic system. Neuromarketers are seeking to understand how to stimulate the buying button in buyers, on demand. Impulse buying contributes to massive spending. Naturally, appealing to this type of buying would be a powerful feature for trade expansion. The University of Twente, in the Netherlands, conducted research on impulse purchases. The research confirmed that the products proximity, time pressure, scarcity, and state of mind are the determining factors when it comes to impulse purchases. Low impact factors were social influence, price, and stock.

One question puzzling the research team was: would neuromarketing be more effective and reliable than surveys and standardized market research methods? Marketers use surveys and market research over decades, to better understand consumer behavior around impulse purchasing.

The question and answer intrigued us. Within standard market research and surveys, marketing teams ask a large cross section of people whether they like the product. If the answer is yes, they ask: will you buy the product, for a certain price? The difficulty with this research approach is that it doesn't consider that the human brain is lying without even knowing it.

This survey method costs the client a lot of money, but arrives at a conclusion they cannot trust. It is astoundingly common that traditional market research methods have an accuracy of just 15 - 20%.

The human brain, both conscious and subconscious, often lies. Now, we can't call all humans liars, and leave it at that, so let's dive a little deeper into this aspect from a neuroscientific point of view. Emotions and non-physical feelings work in close collaboration with each other. Emotions and non-physical feelings are, in a sense, part of the operating system of the subconscious. Reasons, logic, comparisons, and considerations are the operating system of the ratio.

We've established that humans make at least 95% of all their initial decisions emotionally. This implies that when the subconscious makes a decision, the ratio is not immediately aware of it. Worse than that, it doesn't know the subconscious reasoning behind the decision. Feelings cannot translate to trustworthy facts at that moment.

The conclusions reached through neuromarketing research, using an EEG and fMRI, appears to be more reliable than market research with surveys. We've established the process for standard market research, so let's look at neuromarketing research, and draw some comparisons.

To establish a reliable outcome, the researchers only need a small group of subjects. Between 35 and 50 people are enough to gauge the response of the general population. While connected to the fMRI, a product and its price are presented to the subjects. Researchers can determine, based upon where the initial brain activity takes place, if the subject becomes happy when purchasing the product at a certain price.

This will increase the likelihood that they will buy a certain product at a certain price. Researchers can also determine that the subconscious part of the brain decides first, instead of the conscious part.

Three major parts of the limbic system are involved in the decision to buy certain goods at a certain price. The first part of the limbic system worth mentioning is the Insula. It is believed the Insula is involved in identifying, imagining, and processing, many pains. The Insula gives the researchers an indication of the pain created when product and price are presented. The nucleus accumbens is the second part involved. It is believed the nucleus accumbens is related to the rewarding system of the brain. When the nucleus accumbens is activated, by presenting the product, it will increase traffic of neurotransmitters and power flow.

The scientists can determine that the product triggers a certain amount of desire from the subject. As a human, you will feel a desire to own the product.

The level of pain measured in the Insula, and the indication of desire measured in the nucleus accumbens determine the subject's level of interest in buying the product. The question our researchers want answered is: does this subject want to buy this product? When the level of pain is low, and the level of desire is high, the answer is yes. Both areas referred to are running in the subconscious.

The third and final brain part researchers have related to the buying process is the medial prefrontal cortex. It is understood this part makes the final call, based upon several subconscious-driven considerations.

Let's put this into a real-world context. The most popular application of neuromarketing most of us have encountered is in a restaurant. When the waiter gives you the check at the end of dinner, it is offered with candy or chocolate. The idea behind the presentation of the check with chocolate or candy is to disguise the "pain to the brain" which arises by presenting the check. It is crucial to present wrapped candy or chocolate.

Why does it have to be wrapped? This is a simple, but incredibly clever, trick. When the client unwraps the perceived gift, the brain produces dopamine. The dopamine softens the pain of having to pay for dinner. Tests prove that the customer gives a bigger tip when receiving the check with this gift, when compared to when he is presented a check without a gift.

The cortex/neocortex

In common language, the cortex/neocortex is our brain. That makes sense. This part of the brain is responsible for thinking, comparison and reasoning, among other things. This part of the brain houses intelligence, or the so-called higher functions.

The cortex/neocortex formed grooves over time, to improve the volume required to accommodate cognitive tasks. Cognitive tasks are the ability to learn from observations, and the ability to apply that knowledge on demand. The fascinating question is: how powerful is the influence of this brain part, and what role does it play in achieving success?

We now know more about how our brain functions. It stands to reason, then, that it is more important to master the unreliability of the subconscious, than to encourage the brain to become more intelligent.

According to most researchers, the cortex/neocortex is a high-energy consuming part of the brain. It is also very lazy. There is no consensus amongst scientists about the exact speed of the brain in processing information. The subconscious is fast, and low in energy consumption, but very unreliable for reproducing stored information. The subconscious plays a major role in our daily decisions, having a massive influence over our failure and success. To regulate our subconscious decisions, we need our intelligence to understand the difference between subconscious-made decisions which are directed towards our intelligence, and subconscious-made decisions which are not directed towards our intelligence. So, to complicate the process further, when the subconscious doesn't send the information through to our intelligence, what does this mean? It means that we simply *don't know* that we don't know that information.

Lyall Watson posed an interesting dilemma: "If the human brain were so simple we could understand it, we would be so simple we couldn't." Given what you know right now, do you think this is true? And what is intelligence, anyway?

Intelligence is significantly more complex than many people believe. Some people might brag that they are more intelligent than others. Objectively, some individuals are more intelligent than others. But how can you measure intelligence in a reliable way, and how does it contribute to success?

Alfred Binet and Theodore Simon, two French scientists, are the inventors of the original IQ-test. Based on this test, Lewis Terman, a Stanford University psychologist, developed "The Stanford-Binet IQ-test." Even now, this is one of the most common IQ-tests performed, globally. The thing is that our IQ level, as a standalone indicator, does not mean a lot.

You cannot predict someone's likelihood for success in life based upon a high IQ. Intelligence in a distinct area is not always effective, especially if you lack basic intelligence in other areas. Overall intelligence in various cognitive tasks is much more of an indicator. Charles Spearman was the first to develop General intelligence. General Intelligence is widely known as the G-factor.

Raymond Cattell and John Horn took the investigation even further, establishing the theory of fluid and crystallized Intelligence. Crystallized Intelligence is the knowledge you have gathered over time. Fluid Intelligence is the ability to apply this knowledge, and to develop a way to solve problems.

To our personal research and opinion, a valid definition of intelligence is 'The ability of the brain to process, learn, store, and recall information, and apply it at the right moment, in various combinations.'

From a neuroscientific point of view, the compounds and connections in an intelligent brain are more efficient and better organized than in an average brain. A less organized brain consumes more energy, is so much slower in solving issues, and therefore, it is less intelligent.

Can we grow more intelligent during our lives? Yes, we can. The brain can learn and process old and new information at a faster speed. This learning and processing ability, known as neuroplasticity, is not limited to age. It is not yet feasible to calculate what the brain's total storage and data processing capacity is. Some neuroscientists believe the capacity of the brain is large enough to accommodate everything we learn in a thousand year lifespan. Brain capacity is not the obstacle to increasing our IQ.

Scientists believe by increasing the knowledge base—crystallized intelligence—and by applying it—fluid intelligence—our overall intelligence can grow. It will not happen overnight; it takes a lot of hard work, dedication, and determination. The key is to constantly learn new and challenging information, and to consistently practice new skills.

This behavior will change the neurological networks in the brain, and improve your intelligence. Another quick tip: spending more time solving crossword puzzles and playing other brain games, which the brain masters quickly, does not help at all.

8. A healthy brain

As an individual, we cannot look inside our brain in real time. But this just makes it all the more urgent to better understand the basic functioning of our brain. As we all know and understand, preventive measures are much better than creating problems and solving those problems afterwards. Prevention, as they say, is better than cure.

A healthy brain is vital for how we feel, think, and act, and how we behave. A healthy brain is essential for a successful life; whether in private with your family, or in business.

When our brain is in trouble, we are in trouble. We are less happy, less wealthy, less healthy, less intelligent, and we will make poorer decisions. Nobody aims for that lifestyle. The good news is that a healthy brain is, through neuroplasticity, able to repair most of these issues.

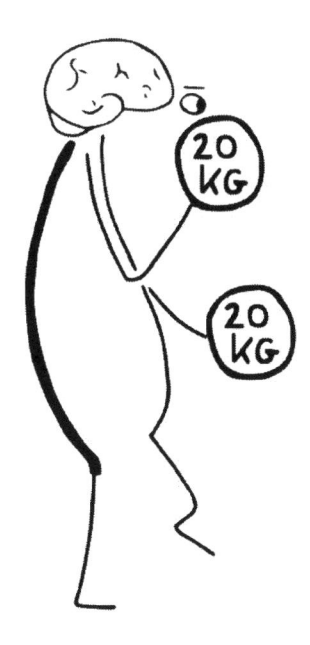

Brainer 8

We might go to the gym or have a regular workout for our body and muscles, but how do we set up a regular workout for the brain? You might know the saying, "a healthy brain is a healthy body," but what do we need to know about our brain? What do we need to do to keep our brain healthy? Can we actually boost our brainpower, and make it more effective and efficient? Next to becoming more intelligent, can we also become smarter, and live a more successful life? If so, how difficult is it to do? Here's the good news: it's not as difficult as you might expect.

The following factors will help tremendously in achieving your goal of having, and maintaining, a healthier brain.

Becoming more successful and maintaining success starts with activating our intrinsic motivation. It simply will not work if we are not absolutely, intrinsically motivated. The key lies in the activation. Everyone is motivated, one way or another. We might want to quit smoking, or give up drinking. We might want to exercise on a regular basis, and have a deep desire for success. Sadly, very few people are able to accomplish their goals. That is not because they are super humans. It's because they have found the activator of their intrinsic motivation. It is nested in their core system of being. They have a deep, core focus on achieving their goal, driven by an emotional subconscious decision.

Thinking about what we want to achieve is not enough. We need to actually feel the reasons, if we want to become intrinsically motivated. In other words, we need to find our personal "Why," which is driven by our subconscious.

Logically, we know that quitting smoking is good for our health. If we are looking for motivation from our ratio only, this is not enough to succeed.

The other important aspect is that we need to know "How" to become smarter, or how to live a more successful life. One of the fundamentals is to know what is healthy, and what is not healthy, for our brain. When we take care of our brain, our brain will take care of us. This knowledge is so essential, in fact, that we have dedicated the next two paragraphs on this topic.

Negative influences on the brain

There are many internal and external influences, measures, and habits, which have a negative impact on our brain. We will only describe the most common situations, because the principles are all the same for the brain.

So, why are we doing so many things that are bad for our brain? Firstly, we don't know any better. Our parents didn't teach us how to care for our brain, nor did our teachers, or society. Secondly, our brain is unhealthy due to poor diet, the constant impact of stress, smog, digital radiation and lack of proper sleep. It's not functioning as it should be.

When our brain is unhealthy, we don't make appropriate decisions, and we do not have the willpower to find out how to do it better. There are some obvious choices that harm our brains, of course. Drugs, nicotine, excessive use of caffeine and granulated or refined sugars, have an adverse impact on our brain functions. Caffeine itself does not dehydrate our body, but it activates the bladder, indirectly subtracting water from the brain. Water is an essential transporter of chemicals, and a catalytic agent of electricity for the brain, so the brain needs it daily, in large, fresh amounts.

Granulated or refined sugars derived from sugar beet and sugarcane are not healthy. Sugar will give the brain a short energy rush. We might feel great and be full of energy for a short period. Too much sugar over prolonged periods can lead to addiction to sugar, loss of control, and an increased sugar tolerance. Almost all western processed foods contain granulated and refined sugars.

Avoiding sugar in our western diets is hard. Very hard.

Granulated and refined sugars do not contain the nutrients we need. They contain high calories and fructose, which our liver will convert into fat. This commonly leads to insulin resistance, heart disease, obesity, and type 2 diabetes. Granulated and refined sugars are empty calories, because they only contain energy and no vitamins, fats, minerals, fibers or proteins.

The World Health Organization (WHO) has set the recommended intake of calories provided by sugar at 10% of our daily food intake. Anything more is considered harmful, if we look long-term, and could have a major impact on our health.

Too much granulated and refined sugars also have a negative effect on the brain. As you consume excessive sugars, your body converts them into fat. As your fat reserves increase, you gain weight. As your body mass index (BMI) increases, less blood flows to your brain. Less blood to your brain means less oxygen. Less oxygen means less nutrition for your brain.

According to Dr. Daniel Amen, the physical size of the brain goes down when the physical weight goes up. Obesity is linked to diseases like Alzheimer's. Have we given you enough reasons to moderate your sugar intake?

Moderate exercise, through sports and fitness, is healthy for the metabolism, and releases our happy hormones. Having said that, some sports are much healthier for the brain than others. We understand that boxing and full contact martial arts, with high impact punches and kicks on the head, are not healthy for the brain. There is also more and more evidence that heading a soccer ball for decades is unhealthy. In fact, all contact sports, specifically sports that involve getting hit in the head, can cause long-term brain damage. Knockouts, like those suffered in boxing matches, can lead to unconsciousness, concussion, and play a major role in brain diseases. That is a no-brainer, so to speak...:)

We are social animals, and like to belong to a group of peers. Ideally, we would belong to a group with shared interests: similar sense of humor, shared sports, fun, hobbies or preferences.

Having said that, this doesn't mean that our friends strive for a healthy lifestyle. Because it is in our biological DNA to belong to a group we will, without registering it, also adapt to the undesirable habits of our group.

We can illustrate this with one of life's most common scenarios: peer pressure. It can be severe. It's so tough to refrain from the wrongdoings of a group, to say "No" to friends who like to get drunk or use drugs when going out. Even if, rationally, we don't want to take part, we still have a biological drive to belong.

It is good to choose your friends and social environment wisely when crafting your personal environment. Hanging out with a healthy peer group with healthy habits can help a lot. Another option is to be a leader, instead of a follower. Choose your personal path; choose health and an enjoyable lifestyle, so that your brain can keep developing its abilities.

Once you have chosen for yourself, your surrounding will change and adapt. You will lose old friends, and new friends will emerge and tag along. Some will stay for a while, others for a lifetime. When you choose for yourself, emotional imbalance between subconscious and conscious will disappear.

A growing illness in Western society is burnout. You might know a colleague, relative or friend who has suffered from this illness, or is experiencing it now. Most often, we do not recognize this person compared to their former self. It is a cruel and dangerous disease, which should be averted at all times.

Another brain illness related to burnout is depression. There is no mutual ground among scientists as to the precise differences between these two illnesses. The general belief is that burnout is work or performance related. Depression, on the other hand, is believed to be more related to self-image, personal relationships, or of genetic origin.

For the purposes of this book, the differences between the two illnesses are not relevant. What we want to focus on is that both illnesses are somehow a conscious choice of the subconscious brain. They both have a significant effect on the health state of the body and brain. They are both extremely damaging to the functioning of the brain. Both illnesses will break down essential nutrients, cell structures in the hippocampus, slowing down thinking capacities and driving emotions to the extreme.

In this state, we can lose neural connections forever. Their attached memories and feelings can even get lost, and never come back. When the brain is in a prolonged state of burnout or depression, negative thoughts will pop up in an uncontrollable manner, day and night.

This could even be a red flag that our body has grown accustomed to high levels of cortisol.

When the cortisol levels are dropping, the body sends messages to the brain. It's almost as though the body is saying, "Please come up with some negative thoughts. Brain, I need you to boost those cortisol levels, so we can feel happy in being unhappy again." A scary fact here is that the brain maintains a vicious cycle to endure the burnout or depression until the issue is resolved. A recent Harvard health study found some thought-provoking causes of depression. The research revealed that the hippocampus is smaller in some people who suffer from depression. An fMRI study published in The Journal of Neuroscience studied 24 women who had a history of depression. On average, the hippocampus was 9% to 13% smaller in depressed women, compared to those who were not depressed. The more bouts of depression a woman experienced, the smaller the hippocampus. Stress, which plays a role in depression, may be a key factor here, since experts believe that stress can suppress the production of new neurons in the hippocampus.

We've established that stress hormones have an important function in our system. Even in a normal, healthy life, we need stress hormones. They are essential to our survival in the face of danger. The part of the brain that regulates these hormones is not very intelligent. It is, however, incredibly fast. Our brain does not make a distinction between being stalked by a predator in the jungle, or in stress mode at work. The brain will produce stress hormones just as readily in our office as it will in the wild.

So, imagine that you leave your house in stress, travel in stress, your workload creates stress, your colleagues create stress, and the cycle repeats all day, every day. The stress then becomes chronic. Chronic stress is dangerous for the brain, and the body.

Chronic stress is a continuous overproduction of stress hormones—your adrenals produce cortisol when in hyper arousal, or as an acute stress response. This is the fight or flight response we know so well, now, making us temporarily stronger, faster and hyper-alert.

When the brain believes it is on an ongoing state of stress, and the cortisol is not being used to fight or flee, the cortisol will remain in our body. In that state, it destroys our body and brain. It prevents intelligent thinking, and leads to increasingly poor decision-making. Bad decisions lead to insecurity, and to more stress. More stress leads to more chronic production of stress hormones. We are caught in a catch-22 situation.

One extremely damaging end to this vicious cycle is adrenal exhaustion. Our adrenal glands cannot produce enough cortisol any longer. To prevent this, we need a better understanding of the vulnerability of the brain. If we want to live a successful and happy life, we need to take care of our brain by reducing our stress levels.

We had interesting discussions with psychologists and burnout consultants who used depression or burnout as the starting point for treatment. Both depression and burnout result from a long path of internal imbalance. Treating the symptoms will never get maximum results. It will take a lot of time, and many setbacks, to recover.

By focusing on and treating the cause of burnout, we have created staggering results over the last few years, and within periods of only thirty to ninety days. This is astounding. Compare this with the two years it can take regular psychologists and burnout consultants to see positive results for their patients.

The neuroplasticity of the brain is huge. New neural connections are made in a relatively short period. This is how a healthy brain is able to cure itself, for the most part, within less than ninety days. To achieve this, we have to meet the exact needs to create balance between the subconscious and conscious parts of the brain. We cannot emphasize enough how essential this is. Research shows that many of our Western illnesses, unhappiness and bad moods are caused by the imbalance between the subconscious and conscious.

We have described negative and positive aspects of cortisol. In our day to day life, our cortisol level is higher in the morning and lower in the evening. Would it surprise you to know that its function is also to wake us up in the morning? Cortisol reduces the sleep hormone melatonin, but in a stressful life, this just causes another interference. During the day, when we encounter many stressful situations, our adrenals keep producing cortisol. Because—hopefully—we do not start a fight or run away, the cortisol level remains in our body. The good news is, if we take time each day to relax, we can decrease our cortisol levels. Lowering our cortisol levels really could be as simple as taking a walk.

Exercising moderately for 30 to 45 minutes a day is the second best thing you can do for your cortisol levels. By moderately, we mean walk, body-walk, jog, rollerblade or cycle—ideally in nature, with many trees to help boost our oxygen consumption. When we live our lives in the fast lane, it is a lot more effective to exercise at the end of the day, instead of the morning.

So, if exercise is only the second best thing you can do, what is the first? Simple. Avoid constant situations of hidden or visible stress. Some people effectively do not accept stress as a part of their lives.

Try to spend most of your time on things you like to do. It will help to lower your level of stress. As a result, you will produce less stress hormones, which will open the door to an increased production of happy hormones.

Positive influences on the brain

Being successful, or becoming successful, is just like being a top athlete. It is hard, disciplined work. A healthy brain is essential for this matter. A healthy brain is also a lot of fun, because it makes life so much easier on all levels. One of the most essential ingredients to a healthy brain, aside from minimizing the negative influences, is to follow your passion. Passion for your hobby, your family life, and certainly for your work, is so important. Confucius said, "Choose a job you love and you will never have to work a day in your life."

This may sound almost too obvious but in real life, we meet too many people who do not follow their passion. In this section, we'd like to walk you through the basic principles for creating a healthy brain.

Our brain needs to have enough fuel to produce positive hormones. So, we need to follow a healthy diet, which contains the right nutrition for the brain. A healthy diet leads to a healthy weight.

There is a narrow correlation between what we eat, how we feel, and how we behave. How we feel has a great impact on the decisions we make. The brain needs constant energy to think. We know that when people are hungry, they are more inclined to say, "No." Hungry people are less sharp than their well-fed counterparts, so they make wrong decisions more often.

Reducing stress is vitally important. It will prevent cortisol levels from rising. A variety of exercises and games play a key role in reducing stress, and challenging our brain. If we do not challenge our brain's intelligence, our IQ drops. Gaming also encourages cohesion between the two brain hemispheres, and makes us more intelligent. You can find tons of these games online.

Research by Professor Siegfried Lehrl, of the University of Erlangen in Germany, shows we lose about 25% of our intelligence during a 4 week holiday period. Some of us won't find this surprising, since we spend much of our holidays sunbathing, swimming, eating and drinking. When we combine dehydration and increased alcohol consumption, our neural connections shrink. To gain intelligence, our brain needs constant challenges.

It is important that our brains learn a diversity of new things, as often as possible. By doing what we are already good at, we are not challenging our brain. We are not improving. Driven by our biological DNA, humans like to improve and create a better version of ourselves. Our brain will cooperate, but only when it finds the new information or improvement relevant.

Regular exercise and movement is important to our general health—and not just for the body. Walking, swimming or bicycling for 30 to 45 minutes a day is more than enough. We do not need to train full force, every day of the week. In fact, top sport is very unhealthy. Our brain will recognize prolonged, strenuous exercise as stress, similar to stress caused by fear. Based on this fictitious dangerous situation, brain and body will jump into stress mode. This will trigger stress hormone production.

The steroid hormone cortisol will even eat our muscle tissue away, if it gets desperate for proteins. This is a major problem for top athletes and bodybuilders, when they do not understand the actual functioning and balance between training, relaxation, food and supplements.

Next on our list of healthy brain boosters: a clean environment and enough sleep are both very important. Sleep is crucial. It allows our glial cells to reset and 'clean' the brain, and enables the stabilizing of neural processes. Young people—between zero and sixteen years old—are most vulnerable here, because we require at least 7 to 8 hours of sleep a night.

A clean environment is fundamental. Many molds are toxic to our brain and body, and they can stay inside of us for decades. Molds from our environment can destroy neural connections in the brain, and prevent the optimal functions of intestines. Speaking of the brain, let's dive deeper into how the parts are functioning.

9. The eight noteworthy brain parts

What are neurons?

Neurons are brain cells. The purpose of a neuron is to communicate internal and shared information with other cells. The receiving cell can be a neural cell or a muscle cell. The size and length of a neuron varies from a tiny fraction of a millimeter to over a meter, due to an extended axon. Now, how do neurons communicate and cooperate? How is information sent from one neuron to another? Neurons use different methods of sending information. To influence the quality of our decisions, we need to understand how sending and receiving of information between neurons works. For starters, neurons communicate in four different ways.

The first one is communication solely through electrical signals. When we want to lift our arm, our brain sends an electrical signal to the muscles in the arm. The muscles will contract and we can lift our arm.

The second one is through an electrical signal activating the release of a chemical signal. The chemical signal will travel to the next neuron, and activate another electrical signal. We'll learn more about this process when we explore neurotransmitters. They play an important role in this process.

The third one is more complex. Thanks to an electrical signal, the neurons will release certain chemicals, like dopamine, for example. Certain areas in our brain house receptors. These receptors are designed to detect and receive dopamine. Once the receptors receive the dopamine, the brain responds accordingly. The amount of hormones we release and the number of receptors varies from person to person. Certain people are more receptive to certain hormones than others.

The fourth one is a theoretical transfer system, but it's still worth mentioning. It is a recent discovery by the University of Copenhagen: transfer by a soliton. A soliton is a single waveform, when compared to a sound form. The soliton will keep its shape and velocity while speeding between locations and carrying data.

Have you ever noticed how, sometimes, your brain and body react instantly? When you make a split second decision, for example, or feel threatened. Or when you burst out laughing in a funny situation. The speed of data transportation through electrical signals is fast. It reaches speeds of up to 120 meters per second. To produce all this electricity, our brain requires a regular supply of fuel: food. Considering that your brain only makes up 1 or 2 percent of your total body weight, it uses an awful lot of your fuel resources.

Our brain absorbs, on average, an impressive 20 percent of all the energy we eat or have stored. In case of an emergency or severe pain, the consumption of energy can increase to as much as 27 percent of our stores.

Really, our brain behaves like a small power plant. It requires a lot of energy to function, and it houses a kind of management system. This internal management system is able to efficiently distribute energy to the areas that need it most. A study by the National Academy of Science USA indicates that two thirds of the brain's energy budget is absorbed by firing electrical signals. The glial cells utilize the remaining 33 percent. When a baby is born, the brain contains around 150 billion neurons. By the age of eight, the brain will prune those 150 billion neurons back to 100 billion neurons. This is still a staggering amount, despite having lost a third of our neurons in eight years. The remaining 100 billion neurons constitute a variety of static and dynamic neural networks.

Each of those neural networks holds or performs a specific task, purpose, thought or behavior. Many brain cells are doing their job around the clock, your entire life.

A lab in Denmark did an experimental gerontology study. The study estimated that if you were to lay all the neurons of one human brain behind one another, the total length of that person's nervous system would be between 120,000 and 180,000 kilometers at birth. By the end of an average lifespan, that length has diminished to approximately 80,000 kilometers.

Synapses

The connection points between neurons are synapses. Researchers at the Salk Institute for Biological Studies calculated that we have around 100 trillion synapses. The number of synapses plays an important role in our memory, the processing of data, and transfer of chemicals.

Glial cells—the maintenance department

When we are engaged in tasks, whether at the office or at home, we create a mess. Mess needs to be cleaned up, or work would stop. The same goes for our brains. The clean-up and maintenance workers of the brain are the glial cells. For a long time they were taken for granted by neuroscientists.

Today we are conscious of these glial cells being vitally important to our brain. The glial cells, the maintenance mechanics of the brain cells, provide crucial support, repair and protection. They clean up dead neurons and other waste. They help keep neurons in place.

They also assist in transporting nutrients and oxygen to the neurons. Glial cells assist neurons to connect with each other through synaptic connections.

Glial cells have so much work to do, that our brain has more of them than it does neurons. Our brain cannot function well without the support of the glial cells.

Brainer 9

An interesting observation is that the ratio's glial cells and neurons might have an influence over someone's intelligence. Take Albert Einstein, for example. His brain had significantly more glial cells than a regular person's brain, and they were packed tighter in the prefrontal cortex. Diamond's 1985 research paper in Experimental Neurology identified one of the four brain samples of Einstein's brain. The sample contained more glial cells for every neuron, compared to a control group of brains.

In 1996, Britt Anderson, at the University of Alabama in Birmingham, published a study on Einstein's prefrontal cortex. He found that the number of neurons was equivalent to brains in a control group, but they were more closely packed. This allowed people to theorize that the closer the neurons are to each other, the faster information can be transported and processed.

Neurotransmitters, electricity and chemicals

We've already pointed out that our brain is a power plant, but it's so much more than that. It's a chemical factory, too. The brain produces chemicals which play an essential role in the communication between neurons. Although each neuron is part of a gigantic network of neurons, most of them do not physically connect. The neuron is just a cell, and each cell has several extensions.

First, let's look at dendrites. A neuron usually has a set of dendrites, which look like the branches of a tree. They receive information, which they pass through to the core of the cell, or across to the next cell.

One of these extensions is not like the other ones, though. It is longer, and has spines on the end. It is called the axon. The axon connects from the core of the cell to specific dendrites, or sometimes to the axons of other neural cells.

At the connection point between the axon and the dendrite, there is a cleft. This cleft is the synaptic cleft. The distance is tiny– between 20 and 40nm small. Information from one neuron has to cross the synaptic cleft to reach the next neuron. Our brain has an ingenious design to accomplish that, which we can examine in its simplest form.

The incoming electrical signal from a neuron converts, through a complex and meticulous system, into chemicals.

These chemicals—neurotransmitters—make the journey from one neuron to the other. Once the neurotransmitter arrives at its destination, it activates an electrical signal, and the journey continues. The actual process is more complex, of course, but we want to give you an overall view of the neurotransmitters function, and the role they plan in our brain. As we write this, over 50 different chemicals have been discovered at work inside the brain. We might discover new ones—there is still a lot to learn.

Besides the technical functions of neurotransmitters, it is crucial to understand their roles and influences on our behavior. The process of transforming electrical signals into chemicals, and then back into electrical signals, is complex, very refined and fast. Neuroscientists call this 'firing.' Electrical signals need to activate new neural connections or networks, or 'wiring.' This complex biochemical microenvironment is subject to mistakes. These mistakes are called 'misfiring.' Misfiring occurs when a signal is not getting to the right destination.

Our brain sometimes comes up with false conclusions. This drives us to act inappropriately, make trivial decisions, or tough mistakes. It does not take very much to go wrong in the initial transfer between the electrical signal and the neurotransmitter. Even a tiny shortage of chemicals will do the trick.

Even when neurotransmitters make the crossover successfully, they might not settle properly. A lot has to do with what we eat and drink, and our lifestyle.

Negative elements—medication, drugs, poor diet, lack of exercise, lack of water, excessive use of alcohol—have a major impact on these micro dynamic rules. If you want to be on top of your game, it's time to live healthy, live smart, and learn more about your brain functions.

Cholesterol the smart maker

Our brain consists of approximately 60 percent fat. Some of us learned the dogma that all fat is harmful and we need to ban fat from the menu. Consuming more than three eggs a week was unhealthy due to the cholesterol levels in eggs. How did this popular idea about fat and cholesterol emerge? The misconception about fat and cholesterol came into the world through a researcher named Ancel Keys. He conducted a study, known as the Seven Countries Study, in 1958. The countries involved were: USA, Finland, (former) Yugoslavia, Japan, Greece, Italy and the Netherlands. Keys presented his results at the World Health Organization (WHO) in Geneva in the early nineties.

The main conclusion of his study was that "saturated fat," found in animals and eggs, caused cardiovascular heart diseases. His study was, according to some contemporary scientists, not conducted well. Even if that was true, the harm was already done. The message was out, and the world was accepting it. Even Governments and health organizations recommended low-fat diets for everyone.

What we now know is that "polyunsaturated fat" helps to reduce bad cholesterol levels in our blood. There are different cholesterols. We will briefly discuss two of them; LDL (low-density lipoprotein), and HDL (high-density lipoprotein). LDL is considered the "bad" cholesterol, and HDL the "good" one. As we're about to see, this is not accurate.

A too high level of LDL will obstruct the arteries. The main function of the HDL variant is to clean up the remains of LDL cholesterol in our veins. So, in fact, they play a part in reducing the risk of heart disease and cancer. Without going too deep into this, the ratio between the LDL and HDL cholesterol is important. This ratio is the difference between being at risk of heart attack, or not. Oils rich in polyunsaturated fats provide us with ingredients that are essential to our body, cell structures and brain. These are omega-6 and omega-3. Because our body does not produce omega-3 or 6, we need to supplement this. Fatty fish like salmon, mackerel, herring and trout, as well as avocados, walnuts and several other nuts, contain this valuable omega-3 and -6.

Cholesterol plays an important role in our brain. Our brain is composed of a higher cholesterol level than any other organ. We find around 25 percent of the body's cholesterol in our brain. Cholesterol serves as crude material to build hormones like progesterone, estrogens, cortisol, testosterone and vitamin D.

A low level of healthy cholesterol increases the risk of depression, and in extreme cases, death. Cholesterol also plays an important part in securing the cell membranes. It simplifies the prompt transmission of the electrical impulses that govern thinking, movement and sensation.

Blood, Oxygen and Water

Our brain needs blood to transports nutrients, oxygen and water, and to flush out dead and toxic materials. About 20 percent of all our blood is needed by our brain. Our brain also requires about 20 percent of our entire intake of oxygen and food.

The oxygen is necessary to provide energy. In this regard, oxygen is the spark of our lives. Just like a fire cannot burn without oxygen, our brain cells cannot produce electricity without oxygen.

As with many other organs, our brain simply cannot survive without oxygen. The website spinalcord.com claims that after only 30 seconds without oxygen, brain cells get damaged. In less than 3 minutes, a lack of oxygen will lead to permanent brain damage. After 4 minutes, death or lasting brain damage become inevitable.

Water also plays an important role. A deficiency of water means reduced oxygen delivery by the blood. Oxygen, as we have just established, is vital to our brain health. When there is an optimum level of water, proteins, vitamins and minerals available, ill health will still exist if there's an oxygen deficiency. That is why proper breathing is so important. It is not uncommon for adults to suffer from shallow breathing. Shallow chest breathing, especially, gives rise to an oxygen deficiency.

Professor Alison McConnell claims that breathing training means applying scientifically validated principles of training theory to the muscles of respiration. Countless research about the importance of breathing in the right way can be found in the pages of the world's most prestigious scientific journals. The quick tip here: do not underestimate your oxygen intake.

Do we eat for our body or for our brain?

A well-known Dutch neuroscientist, Dr. Swaab, declared, "We are our brains." Although it might sounds like an unusual claim, we agree with his statement. Our body is, to put it bluntly, a transportation device to move our brain from A to B.

Our brain requires a lot of energy. Without enough brainpower, we cannot function as a human. When we eat the right brain food, our memory, span of attention, sleep, motivation, and mood, will all improve. There is much at stake. Your brain considers itself the most important organ in your body. If we want to go a step further, out of the three major brain parts, the brainstem considers itself even more important than the cortex/neocortex. Our brainstem controls a considerable part of the energy distribution to the different brain sections.

Now what goes on if we do not eat the right, nutritious, ingredients? Detecting a shortage of energy, the brainstem will redirect all the energy available to itself. It must, among other tasks, secure the breathing, body temperature, heartbeat and respiration.

When the brainstem decides there is not enough energy for the whole brain, it will put the cortex/neocortex on slower speed, because the cortex/neocortex uses a lot of energy. When the brain switches to this mode, we are less sharp, much slower in thinking and responding, and we find it hard to focus. So what do we do to solve the problem? Well, in the Western world, we would normally have a cup of coffee with some refined granulated white sugar.

Researcher Dave Asprey shows us that the brainstem sees white granulated sugar as a very unreliable source of energy. It reacts by slowing down our thinking, and storing the energy in the well-known fat regions, like the belly and thighs, for later use. Besides us not wanting to be less sharp there is another impact on our behavior. If we go back to earlier chapters, we'll remember that our "resistance" is in the brainstem, and our "perseverance and willpower" is in the cortex/neocortex. The effect of consuming too much granulated and refined sugar is that we are less able to pursue our dreams and goals.

The part of our brain that drives our tenacity is on hold. Now we can see why it is important to eat for your brain, when almost everyone else is trying to eat for their body.

Our brain needs many different "nutritious ingredients" to produce all the chemicals it needs. Without a consistent and reliable supply of these chemicals, we feel less happy. We become prone to mood swings; we can't think straight; we can't think fast. We might experience severe difficulties with learning, remembering, and goal setting.

The cooperation between stomach and brain is meticulous. To make sure we feel hungry or satiated, two hormones travel from brain to stomach, and vice versa.

There is a quick point worth remembering: just because we've eaten *enough*, doesn't mean we've eaten *well*. Think about the last time you ate fast food. We can consume a lot of it, but the nutritional value is low. We can be full, but the hunger soon returns. By 'eating well,' we are referring to quality nutrition, vitamins, and minerals.

The two hormones important in this process are ghrelin, which creates hunger, and the peptide hormone leptin, which lets us know we are full. We can notice how this process works when dessert arrives; we can often still find a little place in our stomach for it. Once our brain "sees" a lovely desert, it will immediately signal that there is still some room for this wonderful "gift" presented to us. This response is called: melanocortin-4 receptor–regulated appetite.

The myth that we only use 10 percent of our brain

It would be great news if we only used 10 percent of our brain. Imagine the opportunities if we could find the master key to unlock the remaining 90 percent. That would give us an unfair advantage over other living creatures that could not.

We would understand how other people think, and we could predict and anticipate their reactions. We could remember everything we've ever read, heard and seen. By using this superpower, we could become exceptionally rich, and accomplish everything we want in life. A dream too good to be true, but an intriguing concept for humankind.

Maybe this myth was driven by our desire, as a race, to be the most smart and invincible. Maybe it gives hope to the idea that once we have learned how to access this power, we can overcome every unthinkable threat we could ever face; threats like sickness, aging and mortality. The thought that we can 'beat' these things reassures us, and makes our brain happy.

Hollywood has used this theme in many movies. The main character gets access to the remaining 90 percent capacity of the brain. Some of us might have seen the movie "Lucy." Lucy, played by actress Scarlett Johansson, takes a blue synthetic substance called CPH4 and gains access to 100 percent of her brain's capacity. "Limitless," with Bradley Cooper and Robert De Niro, is about pills that trigger limitless brain capacity. These drugs give direct access to all its' characters brainpower, and make them instantly and exceptionally intelligent.

We all wish these kinds of drugs were available, don't we? Unfortunately, they are not. The myth goes way back.

One interpretation is that scientists found that 10 percent of our brain's capacity is made up of neurons. The other 90 percent were other cells and tissue, like the glial cells we talked about earlier. Scientists believed that the glial cells only had a passive role. With the understanding we have today, we know glial cells do a lot more, and are essential in making our brain function.

The common belief amongst scientists is that we have access to all of our brain, all the time, but that we do not use all of our brain cells at the same time. Using the whole brain at the same time would imply that all the brain cells, i.e. neurons, would fire together. This requires so much energy that it would be almost impossible to accomplish.

From a technical point of view, it is unnecessary to use all of our brain capacity at the same time. We use our visual cortex to see, but not while we sleep, for example.

We use our anger sometimes, but not all the time. We love sometimes, but not all the time, and we use our sense of taste sometimes. Therefore, we have access to all of our brain capacity. The hope of getting access to extra brain capacity, from a current scientific point of view, is futile.

We believe there is another approach to accessing extra brainpower, however. It is a much better way to learn and understand how our own brain, and those of the people around us, operate. The advantages and benefits are exponential.

10. Brain laws revealed

So, we've talked about the basic ingredients and general overview of the brain, all crucial to better understand how the brain operates. We have oversimplified, of course, and left out some important brain parts and their functions. We have taken quite a few shortcuts. We have made a deliberate choice which information to use, so that you have the tools you need to apply your new knowledge to every area of your life.

During our years of research, we talked with many scientists, neurolab researchers, DNA scientists, psychologists and several university professors. Scientists, and especially neuroscientists, use a lot of fancy jargon, and a lot of Latin. Hippocampus, Thalamus, Hypothalamus, brainstem, limbic system, cortex and anterior cingulate cortex are the simple ones. Using Latin words would make this book dull. Even worse, our brain would fail to recognize the relevance of the information and you would stop reading.

The other challenge was that scientists focus on finding the cure for different brain diseases, like Alzheimer's disease, Asperger syndrome, Tourette syndrome, or Parkinson's disease. How to apply this knowledge in a business world is not their primary goal. We have spent more than four years filtering through their data, translating fragments of what neuroscientists know into understandable English.

We have used their combined expertise to create around 200 different brain laws. These brain laws are easy to understand and apply in your everyday life. The results are massive.

We use the term brain laws because, in every country around the world, laws apply to everybody. The brain laws we are writing about are a set of rules by which the brain operates.

This set of rules is part of who we are as humans, and it's embedded in our basic brain functioning. For example when an explosion occurs, everybody gets scared instantly.

Now, 200 brain laws sound like a lot. For you to get the most benefit, we have clustered them into different categories. There are separate brain laws for sales, for communication or leadership, for change management, or making departments work together. Brain laws for maintaining a sound and healthy relationship, or educating your children. Brain laws for high performance organization, motivation, and so on. For each of these topics, we can apply eight to twelve specific brain laws. By knowing a dozen brain laws, you can transform your private and professional world exponentially.

Brainer 10

We have tested our brain laws for many years. Theory is interesting, but practice is often much more unruly. That is why we have gone through a considerable amount of testing of our brain laws. We are fortunate to advise companies with large workforces, and we've had the good fortune to experiment extensively on all social layers, backgrounds and education, for almost four decades now.

Almost all the brain laws we have put to the test worked instantly. A few of the rules, however, we misinterpreted at first, and they had to be adjusted and refined until they gave us the outcomes we were striving for. At first, we thought brain laws were only going to work for higher educated people. We were wrong.

The advantage of the method we have developed is that everyone can learn to apply brain laws. Even children can do this. The fundamental element necessary in learning, understanding, and applying brain laws is intrinsic motivation. Without intrinsic motivation, the brain is unwilling to learn or change and as a result, no new information will be recorded.

Brain laws won't tell you what to do, or what not to do. They offer you the special ingredients you've never heard of, to create your ultimate life. These ingredients contain information on how the brain works. Your brain is intelligent enough to select the information you need, and it will disregard the rest.

The information, which your own brain will select, will unlock the wisdom that is already present inside it. This is how your brain can bring you the success you are seeking. It is the reason we have called our company SparkWise—Sparkling Wisdom. Your brain already contains sparkling wisdom, but it cannot always find the bridge between the right questions and the right answers. This creates the notorious disharmony between subconscious and conscious.

We will not give you an overview of all 200 brain laws in this book. What we will do, over the next several chapters, is give you six basic but essential brain laws. These six brain laws link to each other and are applicable in a great variety of situations. By using and testing these brain laws, you can feel and experience change in many areas: in your role as a parent, in your role as a spouse, in your role as a manager or coworker, in your role as a leader, researcher, teacher, educator, and so on. What we're saying is: you can use these laws in every situation where you deal with your own brain and those of others.

11. The law of intrinsic motivation

Let's start this chapter by explaining why the law of intrinsic motivation is so very important. This brain law gives us one of the essential ingredients for success and happiness. Mahatma Gandhi puts it like this: "Happiness is when what you think, what you say, and what you do are in close harmony." The crucial question is how to activate your own intrinsic motivation, or that of others? This is easier said than done. It can be virtually impossible when you haven't been to brain school yet. Generally speaking, there are two types of motivation: extrinsic and intrinsic motivation.

Brainer 11

People do not like negative situations—in fact, we'll do almost anything to escape them. We humans like to improve ourselves, and hold on to what makes us happy. This is the basis for intrinsic motivation, which resides in our biological DNA. Intrinsic motivation is more far reaching than just liking what you do.

External sources, such as a good grade, positive report, successful experiment, bonus, new experience, reward, a positive rating, or a pat on the back, are extrinsic motivations. Intrinsic motivation is many times stronger and more durable than externally imposed motivations. That is why we will focus on how to find your own intrinsic motivation, and how to trigger that of others. We have developed a very successful method with specific guidelines to activate intrinsic motivation. We will not discuss the different aspects of extrinsic motivation in this chapter.

Our own intrinsic motivation

Why is it so important to know our personal "Why"? To know and feel what we love to do in life, and what fits our personality? How do we get to know this? How can we be sure that what we think we like, is not just a projection from our parents or educators? Some people search for their entire life to find answers to these questions. You're about to discover that the answers are easy.

DNA determines to what extent we produce hormones, and how sensitive our neural receptors are to specific hormones.

This interaction defines who we are as a person, and defines what makes us happy or unhappy. If how we choose to spend our lives is not in alignment with our DNA, unhappiness is lurking on the horizon.

An additional complication is that the intelligent brain cannot "read" our DNA. That is why we as individuals rarely know what makes us happy or not. Unfortunately, in the past humans had to experience and learn all of this by trial and error. Some people pay a high price to find their personal revelations. The older we become, the more life experience we have. The better we know what satisfies us. We are no longer children, without enough life experiences to know what we do, and don't, like. Sometimes, though, even as adults we don't know which direction to go in life. It feels good to know where your passion lies, and it is crucial to becoming, and staying, happy.

When we spend most of our time doing activities that, as a matter of speech, we are made for, it gives us energy. Just like an artist or musician who can work 12 hours a day without getting tired. Spending too much time on activities we do not like will drain the energy out of our brain and body. A natural correlation exists between activities we are good at, and activities we like.

When we ignore the fine balance between time spent on activities we like and do not like, we will end up being unhappy. When we are not happy, we are less successful, and we make big, bad decisions. As a result, we might suffer from illnesses, and are more likely to die sooner than our happy counterparts. Therefore, it is smart to stay as close to ourselves as possible.

Our subconscious is on guard, and will do almost everything in its power to let us know when we are on the wrong track. It starts with small indications. In this process, it will start undertaking activities to sabotage our well-being, gaining increasing traction up to the point of burnout, and in extreme cases, suicide. We will explain this in more detail, and give you some useful guidelines in the chapter "The law of the time balance healthy spends," or to put it in other words: "how a frustrated subconscious leads to sabotage."

It is sometimes very hard to distinguish between DNA-determined intrinsic motivation, and external (educators) programmed behavior. However, this distinction is important because DNA-determined motivation cannot change, whereas programmed behavior can. For some people this quest takes a lifetime, as we're about to see.

We had a client who was the sales director of a big company. He believed that he was a true salesperson, so he told us. Sales were "in his blood," his family and friends always said. The strange thing was that throughout his career, he could not focus on selling a specific product for more than three or four months. He would lose interest, lose energy, and go in search of another challenge—a new product. We had him do a biological DNA test. To his amazement, the results showed that his DNA-driven system was more focused on social relations than sales. In fact, he was not a salesperson at all, by heart. After some digging, we uncovered that as a child, his parents had told him he was a real salesperson, and, in his mind, it became his personal truth. The result was clear: he took over 40 years to find out who he really was.

When we debriefed with him after the DNA assessment, he said, "Incredible, now I have seen the results of my biological DNA, it is crystal clear why I have always felt unhappy and, at some point, even insecure about who I was. Although I have always done my best to succeed, somehow it never felt good enough for my internal system. It would only cost energy instead of creating energy. It is weird to conclude after so many years that it has always been biologically driven. Somehow, because of social pressure, I never listened to my subconscious. I wished that this technique would have existed many years ago. I have wasted so much energy over time. Thank you so much for this eye opener."

After the conclusion, he went to the shareholders of the company and negotiated another position. Today he is a B2B Client Service Director within the same company, servicing, linking, and connecting clients. More importantly, he is one of the happiest people you could ever meet.

Triggering intrinsic motivation of other people

This chapter describes our recommendation, from a neuroscientific point of view, on how we should lead coworkers. Our vision affects current leadership and general management methods. History shows us that most dictators aim to "Divide and conquer." They base their power on creating as much anxiety as possible. The rule they issue is simple: do as I say, or die.

The same system was used, to a certain extent, in the commercial world for many years. It appears a simple and viable strategy, to condition people and keep them in a fear state. It works well when the people you are trying to discipline have no access to knowledge. In current society, with instant access to knowledge through our digital devices, it is significantly more complex to maintain that directive way of ruling. It is obvious that in the long haul it does not activate the intrinsic motivation of coworkers at all.

We have moved over from an industrial-driven society to a knowledge-driven society. We currently have access to knowledge every second of the day. Disruption by the rapid technological innovations is high. What was "hot" yesterday is "not," today. The time in which that happens could be a mere six to twelve months. As a result, managers today are challenged to understand and know everything. Power is shifting. More power lies with the individuals who are experts in their particular field of expertise.

Individually, these experts are not powerful enough to shift a company's mission and vision. But by working together, they can rule a department—sometimes even the entire company. Our current demanding market has changed Management. Smart leaders support coworkers, empowering them with instruments and expertise to improve on a personal level. Successful leaders master the fine art of activating intrinsic motivation of coworkers. We will provide you with five powerful components that you can use to activate the intrinsic motivation of others.

The first component is leading by asking

Management divides tasks between coworkers. Asking each one how they will solve their own challenge and reach their deadline, is more effective than directing them to operate within a certain timeframe. If you are dealing with your organization's quotations department, for example, you'll be more effective asking when they will have a quotation ready for client X, rather than telling them you needed client X's quotation yesterday. By using the asking technique, individuals will find their own arguments and commitments. We use this technique in sales and conflict management, but it is sound and valuable for any manager. Using specific, targeted questions will stimulate self-determination, in turn motivating coworkers to feel more confident in creating and applying their own solutions.

The second component is about money

We were curious: Is money sufficient motivation for us to commit to a task? Research reveals that money only motivates temporarily, under specific conditions, and in certain situations. Therefore, it is important to understand what works for the brain.

As we learned in the quick section about dopamine, a short-term reward works much better than a long-term bonus. A modest weekly bonus, for instance, will motivate people much better than a higher annual bonus. It doesn't matter that the annual bonus is considerably higher than all the weekly bonuses combined.

The third component is about time value

Our brain understands that time is limited. We can only spend it once. There is not a shop, bank, or institute where we can buy extra lifetime. That is why your brain appreciates the effort when someone gives you personal attention. In this situation, your brain produces positive hormones and, as a result, it will become more receptive, and less critical. Are you ready for a quick tip? When you have a problem to solve, need support for an idea, or need a coworker to do something – do not email them. Go and spend time with them. The impact this has is astounding.

The fourth component is about gamification

Gamification is effective as a weapon to overcome resistance. Turn your idea, new goal, or situation into a game—a competitive game. The prize can be anything from a cake to an honorable mention, but it should be a public reward to create status within the group. Winning produces positive hormones and stimulates individuals to perform better. A client of ours recently implemented this component with great success. The challenge for users was to find bugs in the beta version of a new software. The person finding the most software bugs was the winner. Using the new software was straightforward, and within a month all the bugs were worked out.

The fifth element is about positive group pressure

Most individuals love to be part of a group. To deviate from the general vision of a group will cause pain in the brain. To apply this technique, it is important to concentrate on the informal leaders within the group. Once you convince them, the rest will follow much more willingly. A common mistake managers make is putting a lot of time and effort into trying to win over each individual opponent within a group. They are underestimating the power of those in the group that support their vision. When the supporters confront the opponents with social group pressure, basic resistance is diminished, and cooperation is the result.

Positive hormones are essential to activate intrinsic motivation. Modern leaders should invest more time in understanding the importance of this biochemical process, and how it influences behavioral change, and flows on to success.

Intrinsic motivation, though, is not the only ingredient we have to play with. The other vital ingredient is self-determination.

12. The law of self-determination

Self-determination is a crucial and intriguing law. This law is needed to activate intrinsic motivation. We cannot separate the law of self-determination from the law of intrinsic motivation. Some of the elements we use to activate intrinsic motivation, for example, also apply to the law of self-determination. Although there are several similarities between these two brain laws, there is also one big distinction.

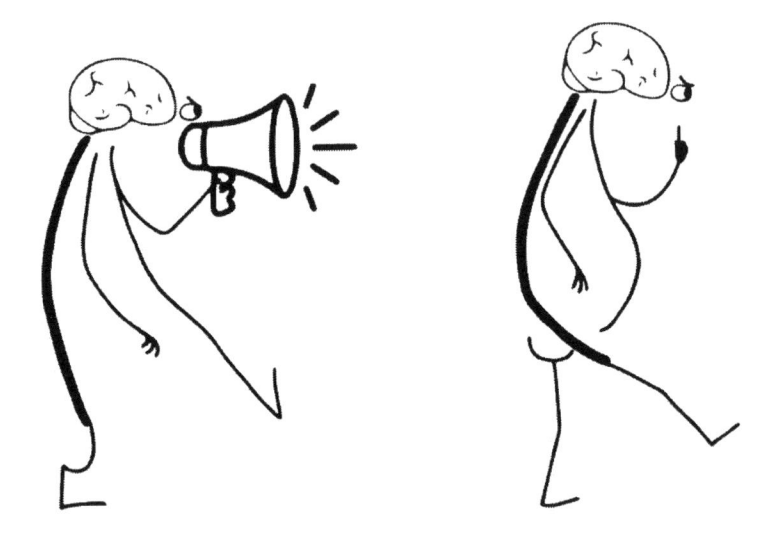

Brainer 12

Our intrinsic motivation is diminished when a (too) strong external compulsion is imposed. Any kind of external coercion, pressure, or 'should or must do,' lowers our self-determination. This can lead to a situation in which our intrinsic motivation is high, but our self-determination is low. When faced with this situation, we are not likely to cooperate. Stimulating self-determination in others is a hard task, but it is possible.

It is difficult to do because it is in the brain's nature to believe its own perceptive truth. The brain uses the archive system as its source of reference. Based on these reference points, the brain creates internal orders and directions. As a logical result, we are all inclined to impose our own truth onto others. This drives us to disregard the law of self-determination of the person receiving our message.

The automatic impulse to impose our own perceived truth upon others is a mechanism, controlled by the subconscious brain. It is a powerful mechanism, and it takes a lot of practice to change. What we need is brain-friendly communication. Fortunately, by using the latest neuroscientific knowledge, we have invented that.

How to stimulate self-determination

We've all been in a situation where we've asked someone, politely or not, to do something. They say, "Sure, I'll do it," which convinces us that they will do it soon. From experience, we know that this isn't always the case. Especially within a hierarchy, often the part of the brain that wants to give socially desirable answers has given the answer: "Sure, I'll do it." We can't trust this answer, but how do we respond? Is it wise to get upset because your request was not executed as promised? What if, instead of getting upset, you learned to use more effective, brain-friendly communication to get what you want?

It's tempting to get upset when someone says "YES" but does "NO." This kind of reaction—getting upset—might work for a parent or a leader in the short term, but not in the end. It is crucial to remember that when you take someone's self-determination away, you are increasing the risk of that individual sabotaging the task.

The sabotage can range from very subtle and hard to detect, to blatantly confronting and transparent. Either way, the impact can be huge. Let's examine two valuable techniques that will help you to avoid these issues at home, at work, and everywhere in your daily life.

The asking questions technique

In the previous chapter—intrinsic motivation—we described how to use an asking technique to activate intrinsic motivation. The law of intrinsic motivation is very much linked to the law of self-determination. So, if you thought you could apply the asking technique to this brain law, you'd be right. To illustrate, let's explore two examples of using the asking technique in different situations.

Firstly, suppose you have a challenge. The challenge might be a deadline that is not workable in your current working environment. Or, on a personal level, maybe you have an adolescent daughter trying to manipulate their curfew so that she can come home later.

A brain-friendly technique will leave the self-determination intact. It will not tell the people involved what to do. It will ask them how they would solve the problem themselves. At this stage, we need to be prepared for the solution to be slightly different than what you had in mind. Still, chances are much higher that they will do as promised.

Sticking with the example of the adolescent and her curfew, let's look at a brain-friendly approach. First, sit, talk, and let her know that you'd like to treat her as an adult-in-progress. You could say:

"As an adult in progress, it is logical that you are taking responsibility for yourself. It's biologically driven, and I understand that, but with new freedom comes new responsibility. So, what time would you like to come home?"

It is important to actively listen to her responses, and to reply calmly. You could respond with, "All right, let us say that somehow, for whatever reason, you cannot make it in time; what will be the punishment if you do not keep your promise? I'll give you two options: either you cannot have your phone for two days, or you do the housekeeping, dishes and garden for the next 5 days."

At this stage, you'd probably be hoping she would be late, for the free housekeeping and maintenance...:) Be very strict when you apply this system, because many people, adolescents and adults alike, will try to come up with a third option that suits them better.

The second example brings us to another important feature of the brain. Our brain loves to decide; the easier the choice, the quicker the decision. Even if there is no specific need for the decision, it is still easy to seduce the brain into deciding on something.

Despite our brains' love for decision-making, it is not all that demanding of concrete facts and hard evidence. As if that isn't bad enough, it doesn't always use the right information to decide, either.

Business and sales apply this decision-making technique daily. To the brain, there is a big difference between asking:

- Do you like our products?

Or

- Which of these two products do you like the most?

The first question leads to a "yes," "no," or "maybe" answer. When you receive a "no," you are back at square one.

The second question helps your brain to choose between the two products on offer. The next example illustrates how easy it is to seduce the brain.

In our master classes, we show a text that describes a fictitious person, and based on the text provided by us, our participants have to make a choice. The choice they have to make is to decide whether our fictitious person is a farmer or a librarian. What amazes us is that everybody will make the choice. Over the decades we have been asking this, nobody has ever said: I do not have enough information to make that decision.

The next question we ask in these workshops is: what evidence, information or facts do you need to determine whether she is a farmer or a librarian? This leads to quite a discussion amongst our participants. It is common for them not to agree on a list. They do agree, however, that they do not solely rely on the text we give them to make a solid decision. This exercise illustrates to our participants how easy it is for the brain to tempt the brain to make subconscious-based snap decisions.

How self-determination can lead to bankruptcy

The law of self-determination can cause problems on a different level. Self-determination sometimes prohibits individuals from embracing progression. Signs of progression, like fast changing technology and market conditions, are external factors. They are not initiated by the person involved. Being that they aren't something we ourselves initiated, they activate instant resistance on a subconscious level. It is difficult for the brain to adapt to changes in such conditions. When the brain believes a proven strategy or structure was successful in the past, it likes to hold onto that belief.

We have developed certain techniques over the years, to overcome this problem. With these simple techniques, we help the most stubborn brains to understand that their beliefs have become obsolete, and are no longer relevant to our time and era.

Senior management is notorious for holding onto obsolete beliefs. Imagine for a minute that old school management of an organization has difficulty keeping up with the disruptive changes in modern society. Statistics show that they are losing client loyalty, so sales are dropping. As Albert Einstein so eloquently put it, "We cannot solve our problems with the same thinking we used when to create them." Changing a manager's way of thinking implies that almost all management must change their way of thinking. That could just be a bridge too far.

It is almost impossible to find a solution to this problem, keeping the two brain laws of intrinsic motivation and self-determination in mind. We recognize that swift action is required, but acting against the two brain laws might lead to an undesirable outcome. So, what to do?

Back in 1997, the millennium challenges started. We created a system that we called: create a secret Ninja society. Nowadays, this approach is widespread internationally, but it's known as: create a cannibal. It sounds unorthodox, but it is more or less based on the well-known quote from Harry Truman: "If you can't convince them, confuse them."

Here's how it works:

Set up a small corporate subsidiary or spin-off (NEWCO) with a fair budget. Fill management positions with motivated, ambitious, preferably young, intelligent, rebellious, creative, out-of-the-box thinkers. Select them from both in and outside the business branches. Give them only one designated purpose: Beat the mother company with all possible means, within the shortest timeframe possible.

An important requirement for success is to give Carte Blanche to the management team of the cannibal. They do not report to the mother company's board of directors, for example. Therefore, the NEWCO does not deal with the organization's established management layers. They can experiment with, test, and push through new ideas fast.. They can make use of social marketing and growth hacking skills to build their brand fast. They can cut deals with competitors to reach their goals fast. Without the usual internal policies and regulations of the mother company, everything can move fast.

And through all of this, the mother company gathers substantial new information to decide which direction to follow.

13. The law of relevance

Let's talk about the law of relevance, which we'd like to add to your toolbox. Relevance largely determines whether your brain will listen, pay attention and learn. Being the curious individuals that we are, we have questions about the implications and applications of this brain law. How do we know what is relevant to someone or not? How can the law of relevance help us to get people to change? How can we use the law of relevance to increase sales? Has modern technology, like smart phones and social media, had a big impact on the law of relevance? How can we deal with this phenomenon?

A lot of questions, right? Fortunately, by filtering through years of research, we can answer them together.

Western society bombards people with offline and online impulses. Estimates show that, at present, our brains have to process around 3,500 impulses per day. In 1916, a mere hundred years ago, we were processing around 150 impulses per day. This disruptive increase in the number of daily impulses poses a serious challenge for our brain. This is a massive amount of data to process every day. Our conscious brain is just not equipped to process this huge amount of information, but it has to deal with the overload somehow.

The skipping and swiping strategy

In order to survive every day, our brain has developed the 'skipping and swiping' strategy. The brain almost automatically 'swipes' the bulk of information as irrelevant. Swiping is our brain's way of saving the energy available for processing information.

Because of this 'swiping' strategy, people have become more superficial. We see the symptoms of this superficial behavior every day. No doubt, you notice it, too.

A perfect example always presents itself when two people are dining together. During dinner, they spend more time chatting with their so-called friends on social media, eyes glued to their phones, than conversing with their dinner companion.

When faced with the brutal efficiency of 'skipping and swiping,' let's explore the opportunities and threats of the brain law of relevance.

The essential question to pose is: what information is relevant, and will overcome the skipping and swiping strategy of the brain? We can answer this question from two different angles.

The first angle is: how can we make sure that our audience notices the information we are sending?

The second angle is: how can we make sure our subconscious brain will catch the important information and share it with our intelligent conscious brain? We can only do something intelligent with information if our subconscious passes this information on to the conscious brain. If it doesn't, all we're left with is a vague "feeling" that we cannot interpret.

Let us start with the first angle. We know existing information in the brain's archive system prevails above the new and sometimes conflicting. This instant defense mechanism is hard to beat, but there are principles we can apply.

How to get noticed

It becomes more difficult to stand out in the huge tsunami of daily information that bombards your audience, and to be noticed with your product or service. This isn't helped at all when we consider that the subconscious brain always decides whether information is relevant or not, within a fraction of a second.

Essentially, we have a very narrow window of time in which to be recognized as relevant. Therefore, "the law of relevance" is more important than ever.

Relevancy is perceived by the brain in a multitude of ways. It recognizes relevance when a threat or dangerous situation emerges. In a positive sense, it recognizes relevance as aiding you in becoming more successful. Similarly, your brain will view information as relevant if it helps you create a better version of yourself.

We know that fear is a very strong impulse for the brain. A fear-driven message is processed much quicker by the brain than a positive message. That is the reason the media creates fear. Cleverly, they are using the law of relevance to compete for our attention. To our brains, fear and negative messages are closely related. If you've ever wondered why you remember the negative pitches, messages, feedback, and advertisements–now you know.

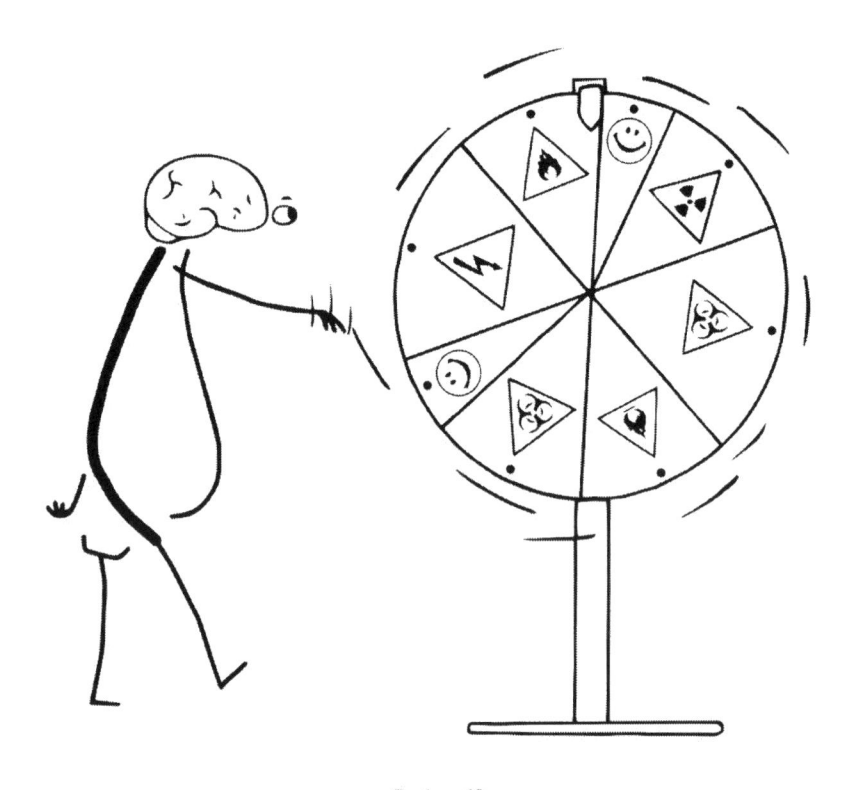

Brainer 13

The possibility of a loss, which an implied negative message, elicits a response to avoid or minimize the risk of loss, rather than the accrual of gain.

In literature, this is often referred to as loss aversion. A good example is how insurance companies use negative messages in their advertisements to sell their services. Insurance companies emphasize the terrible risks of not having life insurance. The insurance companies do not explain that accumulated fees are higher than the total amount that will be reimbursed to you. Many of us would be better off saving that money for 40+ years, instead of paying insurance fees.

We have explained why and how an explicit negative message works, how powerful it is, and its recognized relevance to our brain. Interestingly, the principle of loss aversion also has a huge impact on our behavior at a subconscious level. The problem is that we don't realize this loss aversion mechanism drives us. We do not recognize how it influences our daily performance. In the context of how the brain deals with negative influences, let's explore a couple of compelling examples.

Daniel Kahneman discovered a basic brain principle, loss aversion, in his book "Thinking Fast and Slow"[2]. He explains that loss aversion dictates our daily behavior, the quality of our decision-making, and our level of performance. Our performance level could be higher, he determined, if loss aversion didn't drive us.

A study by Devin G. Pope and Maurice E. Schweitzer is a very nice example of how great the influence of loss aversion is on our performance, and how much money we do not realize we are losing[3]. Pope and Schweitzer have investigated the impact of loss aversion in the game of golf. Their theory was measured on the number of strokes needed before the golf ball was in the hole. They performed the study on golfers of the PGA tour, where the financial stakes are high. They concluded that golfers are less accurate in putting for a birdie or eagle, because of an intrinsic loss aversion, than when they are putting for par or over par. As all golfers know, par is our point of reference.

The analysts of the study calculated that Tiger Woods would have received an extra $1,000,000 a year, had his under par putts been as precise as his par putts. This study was intriguing – imagine what kind of money a pro athlete like Tiger Woods could have earned, had he known the impact of loss aversion.

Determining a standard, or point of reference, based upon how the brain functions, has a tremendous impact on profit realization for any individual or organization. In its simplest terms, loss aversion has a massive influence over our potential earnings.

People expecting to lose, feel most affected by changes. Fear, which manifests as insecurity in this scenario, is recognized as relevant to the brain. Our subconscious manages loss aversion, so you cannot neutralize the fear of loss by using rational facts, arguments or reasoning.

What does help is starting at the root of the problem – the functioning of the brain. It is crucial to help the brain to better understand its own functions. Once the brain understands how loss aversion affects our decisions, we can change.

When we want to get through to our brain, indirect communication is a lot more effective than direct communication. By nature, your brain is creative and curious, and it has a weakness for interesting storytelling. We know this of children and adolescents, but it also applies to us later in life. When we tell a story the right way, the brain becomes curious and wants to listen, to determine the relevance of the story. When the brain expects a level of relevance within the story, it will remain interested until the end. To succeed with this technique, it is important to build the story in successive parts.

Relevance of new learning methodologies

How does modern technology influence our brain's natural relevance-detection system? More than this, how does modern technology impact the learning systems used in our schools, universities, and training agencies? What was relevant, decades ago, is no longer relevant to the brain today.

An example of this phenomenon is the number of phone numbers we used to know by heart. How many phone numbers did you know by heart 20 years ago? Most people of a certain age knew a whole catalogue of phone numbers by heart. Now, most of us are lucky if we remember 5.

The brain knows remembering a phone number is no longer necessary, because our cell phone stores it. The same phenomenon changes the willingness of a coworker or student's brain to learn and remember facts and dates from the past. This new attitude has major implications for how brains learn. As a result, we need to offer brain-friendly teaching materials.

Some companies already use agile, virtual, and augmented reality tools. The impact of modern technology on the relevance of information explains why old learning systems no longer work effectively.

To complement these technology-based learning solutions, we use newer techniques in learning environments. These techniques really open our brains up to adapting and learning. We often use a thematic build up technique. Let's look at how this achieves our goals.

Select three subjects or themes that your audience is interested in. The audience can only choose one theme to work with. The choice activates their self-determination, driving them to choose the topic with the highest relevance. When this technique is applied systematically in an educational environment, the results are impressive. Ask children at a primary school whether they want to learn about dinosaurs, mammoths or dragons. Ask University students of Economics whether they want to explore a case study on Uber, Kodak or the Lehman brothers.

Coworkers in your sales department might want to choose between growth hacking, the KAIT-DR sales model, and brain-friendly communication. The audience selects the topic they feel interested in or passionate about.

This system will create a few positive effects, two of which are:

1. Improved absorption ↓ provided that the curriculum is properly composed, this system is composed in such a way that students or coworkers will much easier learn related disciplines and subjects.
2. Improved recall ↓ because the laws of intrinsic motivation and self-determination are fully respected, the curriculum or material at hand is remembered much better, and retained for a much longer time.

In our earlier example, kids at the primary school were given the choice to learn about dinosaurs, mammoths or dragons. They chose dinosaurs. While learning about their chosen subject, the children had to answer additional questions like: Where, and in which period, did the dinosaurs live? What did the dinosaurs eat? Who were their most dangerous enemies? How did they become extinct? How fast could some of the dinosaurs run? By implementing our system, the kids were able to learn aspects of biology, history, geography, math and other relevant teaching materials, in a natural, brain-friendly way.

Improve your own internal relevance detection system

Why is it important to know how to improve and upgrade our personal relevance detection system? It is important because it can enhance the opportunities we face. We might recognize that some people spot even the smallest of opportunities, while others do not even recognize the big ones. Why?

Well, we've established that our subconscious isn't necessarily passing all received information on to the conscious brain. Whether information is relevant or not is decided by a not-so-intelligent brain part, which uses an inaccurate archiving system. Therefore, some new information, which conflicts with stored information, is dismissed before it arrives in our intelligence. Essentially, this is why people are failing to see big windows of opportunity in their lives. Our subconscious brain isn't pre-programmed to recognize the relevance of this opportunity.

Knowing this, how can we program the brain to notice opportunities?

We often think about what we do not want to do. To our brain, that is a mixed message. Our brain does not process the words "not" or "don't," very well. If we told you right now, for example, not to think of a pink elephant, what would happen? Despite how hard you try, you'll start thinking of this pink elephant. It is hard to delete this thought. When we do not tell the subconscious brain what we want, it does not understand what is important, and it cannot pass on the relevant information.

To help the subconscious brain figure out what is important, we need to do some training and reprogramming. Writing and repeating, creating mood boards, visualizing what we want to achieve – these are all useful techniques to train and reprogram the brain.

14. The law of communication

Brainer 14

Why is convincing other people so difficult? Why are we so devoted to showing people that brain-friendly communication is more effective? What is brain-friendly communication? And most importantly, how do you apply it?

Communication seems easy, but communicating in a brain-friendly way takes practice. It can be hard at first. We first need to explain what the SparkWise definition of brain-friendly communication is. Most people believe communication is the sending and receiving of information. All true, but a crucial element is missing. Verbal and nonverbal communication is all about mutual understanding.

Without mutual understanding, there is no effective communication. Brain-friendly communication is so hard because in order to communicate well, you have to do something that, before starting this book, you might have struggled with. You have to master your emotions.

Why the brain distorts information

Sometimes, you can take time to carefully compose a message, only for the receiver to completely misinterpret it. Why does that happen? Is the other person not listening to you, or is their brain playing a trick? Simply put, yes – the brain is playing a trick. The brain always relies on its own archives. The brain distorts incoming messages in an attempt to fit them into the existing archive system. As a result, the incoming message is misunderstood. If we do not understand this process of distorted information, we assume that the receiver understands our message in the same way we mean it.

Words can also create miscommunication. We advise organizations, from family businesses to multinationals to public organizations to hospitals. Most industries have their own use of words. Industries take normal words, and manipulate them into different meanings that fit the new context. Some words, or whole sentences, might sound decisive when they are actually a disguise to delay decision-making. With a recent client, we came across the phrase, "Tapping a decision." This short sentence gave us the impression that the executives were poised to make a decision. The truth was, none of the decision-makers were poised. It took three months for them to decide on even simple issues.

When we send information, it gets altered by the receiving brain to fit into their individual archive system. This mutual registration and communication system causes a miscommunication. Technically speaking, it's not your fault. You were not aware of this process taking place in your brain, before now.

We all communicate based upon our individual point of view, values, disbeliefs and beliefs. Without realizing, we can put a hidden purpose or judgment in our message.

If we look at some common phrases, we can see this in action. "I disagree with you"; "You have done something wrong"; "What you are saying isn't logical," etcetera. The receiver of your message will go into defense mode, because his brain is now clinging to its own point of view, value, disbelief, or belief. These two forces create a conflict. Humans that communicate this way are doing the complete opposite of what brain-friendly communication achieves.

"Assumptions are the mother of all misunderstandings." At least, that's the clean version of the well-known proverb. It summarizes what we have explained in the previous sections, and is illustrated below, for our visual learners.

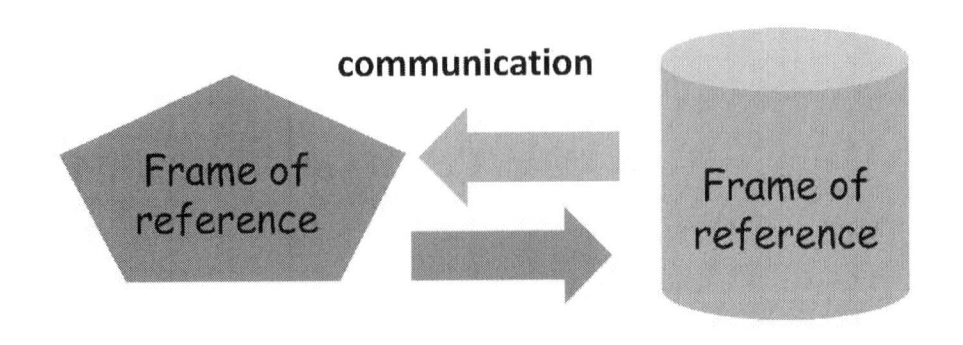

communication

Frame of reference ⇄ Frame of reference

As the sender, you communicate in your individual shape and color, based on your personal archive process. The person receiving your message also has a unique archive process, with a different shape and color. The subconscious brain of the receiver distorts the information you send it, to make it fit with his own shape and color. In this example, the blue pentagram message is sent, and converted into a green cylinder. It is a lot like toddlers trying to put a square peg into a round hole.

The purpose of learning brain-friendly communication in a corporate or private environment is to prevent misunderstandings. Fewer misunderstandings help individuals to behave and operate in a more constructive direction. Applying brain-friendly communication results in less frustration, less conflicts and less fights. It also prevents us from trying so hard to convince others. Less force in this area creates more recognition of different individual opinions.

The most important guideline to implementing brain-friendly communication is to explain the law of communication. Messages can be misinterpreted. Our carefully chosen words sometimes lead to an unexpected response. It takes practice to make the conscious brain detect symptoms of miscommunication, and to guide it to act accordingly. We use gamification to help teams and departments to spot examples of brain-(un)friendly communication. Once the brain learns where it is mis-stepping, improvement follows automatically.

Guidelines for brain friendly communication

As complicated and fraught with booby-traps as brain-friendly communication can be, you can be on your way to achieving it in less than 10 steps.

1. Check if important messages are well interpreted and understood in the same way you intended them.
2. Dispose a value judgment in your message.
3. Make sure you never violate the rule of self-determination.
4. Use the strength of the law of intrinsic motivation.
5. Steer on the production of positive hormones.
6. If you feel your reaction is emotional, share this with the person or group. By sharing it, the intelligent part of the recipient's brain can handle it better.
7. Use social group power to influence others – do not do it yourself.
8. Lead by asking questions. A positive questioning process might look like this.
   Person 1: Is your decision, opinion or conviction based on a feeling or a fact?

   Person 2: My decision is based on a feeling.

   Again, ask a question and offer two options.

   Person 1: Feelings are personal and most of the time not based on facts. Do we A: Increase, or B: Decrease, the chance of making a good decision when appointing facts?

   Person 2: A decision based on facts is probably better.

   Person 1: OK. Let's explore together which facts you need to make a well-balanced decision.

15. The law of healthy time balance

Steve Jobs once said:
Your job will fill a large part of your life, and the only way to be truly satisfied is to do what you believe is great work. And the only way to do great work is to love what you do. If you haven't found it yet, keep looking. Don't settle. As with all matters of the heart, you'll know when you find it.

A life spell, such as that of Steve Jobs, contains certain wisdom, but it can be hard to implement in our everyday lives. We do not always have the luxury, or budget, to keep looking for our dream job. Most of us are facing the harsh reality of a normal life – mortgages, rent, health insurance, groceries, clothes, and holidays with our family. When we look at it that way, you could say we are in perpetual need of money. Sometimes, we just have to accept work we don't like.

The law of healthy time balance, or "how subconscious frustration leads to sabotage," gives a more practical direction for a healthy balance. It shows how much time we should spend on work we enjoy, and on work we dislike.

Subconscious frustration leads to sabotage

We perform a lot of different activities and tasks during the day. Our subconscious uses a special accounting method to calculate the value of those activities. The subconscious categorizes these activities into three different values: enjoy, dislike and neutral.

Value one contains time spent on activities you really **enjoy**. Your subconscious sees these as relevant.

Value two contains time spent on activities you really **dislike**. Your subconscious sees these as irrelevant.

Value three contains time spent on activities you are emotionally **neutral** about. Your subconscious is indifferent to these activities.

On average, we spend around 20 to 25 percent of our time on activities in the neutral category, which is fine. We are indifferent to those activities or tasks – we do not have a heavy emotional attachment to them. It is a completely different story, however, when we are spending around 50 percent of our time on activities we dislike. This triggers our subconscious brain to take strange action. It starts to lump together the time we spend on activities we both **dislike** and view as **neutral**. Suddenly, our emotional conclusion is that we are spending 70 to 75 percent of our time on activities we **dislike**.

The subconscious brain will only accept this status for a short period. When this unhealthy balance lasts for longer than a few months, the subconscious brain will start with slow sabotage. The signals will be small, to start out. If you ignore these issues for too long, however, the subconscious will gradually push you towards exhaustion. This eventually will lead to burnout at work, and massive damage in our personal lives.

It's clear, then, how imperative it is to maintain a positive and healthy balance. SparkWise has developed a practical formula to help you calculate healthy time balance.

Healthy time balance formula

We express a healthy time balance with the following formula:

$$N + E > N + D$$

The **N** stands for **N**eutral, **E** stands for **E**njoy and **D** stands for **D**islike

When our emotions and the subconscious register an unhealthy balance of time spent, a conflict arises between the subconscious and our intelligence. Our intelligence will rationalize. It will justify, demanding its own rights. We rationalize by telling ourselves things like: I have a responsibility towards my family. I have to save money for my pension. I'm doing this to give my wife and kids a good, wealthy life.

These are some of the many justifications we get while treating professionals coping with burnout. But how can we recognize these stress symptoms, while they're still small enough to manage? The great news is: they are easy to spot. They manifest as lesser sleep, lack of energy, and a snappy, disagreeable mood. When we spot these signs, the key is in not letting your intelligence fool you. Listen to the signs. Register your symptoms in a little notebook, or in your phone. Look for a pattern. The best advice is to listen to your subconscious, and to maintain a healthy balance of time spent.

We have another tip for you, too: spend at least 50 percent of your time on activities you really **enjoy**.

Why? Because the formula we looked at earlier works both ways. Using work as an example, consider that our subconscious registers 20 to 25 percent of our time spend as **neutral**.

When we spend 50 percent of our work time on activities we **enjoy**, our subconscious does its strange trick again. It will add up the 50 percent we are spending on **enjoy,** and the 20 to 25 percent spent in **neutral**. The total time spent in **enjoy** mode, according to our subconscious, is now at 75 percent. For some of us, that might be even better than at home…:)

Our brain is very well equipped to spend up to 35 percent of our time on activities we **dislike**. Of course, we all know people who strive for 100 percent fun, all the time. Would it surprise you to know, then, that aiming for 100% enjoyment is not such a great idea? After a reasonably short period, the subconscious will set this new level of happiness as its default setting. It will become less stimulated, and slow the production of dopamine. What we're saying is, do not spend the rest of your life only playing golf and eating steaks.

Psychologists Killingsworth and Gilbert, of Harvard University, wrote: "A human mind is a wandering mind, and a wandering mind is an unhappy mind. The ability to think about what is not happening is a cognitive achievement that comes at an emotional cost."[4] Effectively, a bored brain is not happy. It will act in the same way a brain does in an unhealthy time balance. As a result, depression can occur.

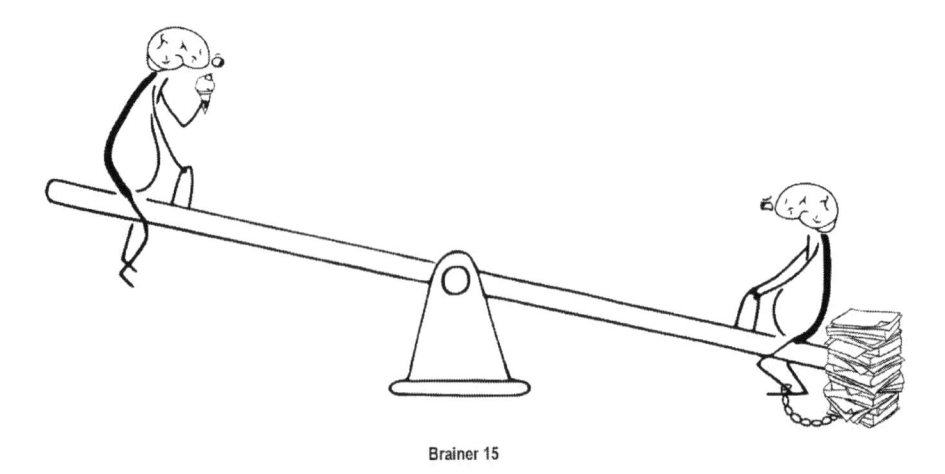

Brainer 15

Guidelines to avoid subconscious frustration

The brain law, "healthy time balance" leads us to three significant guidelines:

1. As a leader or manager, it is our task and responsibility to ensure individuals are spending at least 50 percent of their time on activities and tasks they enjoy.
2. We also need to spend at least 50 percent of our time on activities we enjoy. This takes considerable planning, but decades of experience and research show that we will each be happier and more successful for it. As a fringe benefit, being happier influences you as a spouse, parent, friend, colleague, and boss.
3. Spending up to 30 percent of our time on activities we dislike is essential to maintaining a lively brain.

Determining how to spend your personal time within these three categories is not all that complicated. To start, make a note of where your time is allocated in an average week, honestly and accurately.

We have developed a quick Healthy Time Balance form, which you can download free from our website: http://www.whyofeverything.com/healthytimebalance

Track and categorize your activities for just a week, or a few weeks, to gain insight into where your time is going.

16. Success management based on neuroscience

We have already made it to our final brain law: the law of Success Management. The preceding five brain laws: intrinsic motivation, self-determination, relevance, communication and healthy time balance, are all indispensable elements in achieving success. If Brain Laws were an orchestra, those guys would be the musicians. "Success Management" would be the conductor.

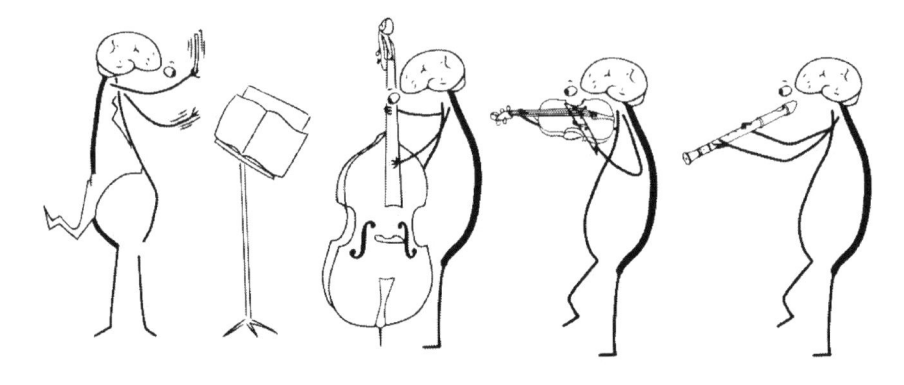

Brainer 16

This conductor uses the musicians, their instruments and music pieces to create symphony. The conductor doesn't necessarily use every musician, or every instrument, at one time. When needed, the conductor brings the music together in harmony and creates the musical performance.

In this section, we'll explore how each of us can be the conductor of our own orchestra. Before we get started, though, we'd like to show you how to prevent your musicians from playing bum notes.

An untrustworthy brain

When astronauts go to outer space, even the smallest mistake can be disastrous. To avoid disastrous mistakes, the military and NASA have conducted several Human Reliability Analysis (HRA) studies and experiments over the years. Alain Swain presented one such development back in 1962. Swain presented a paper introducing a Technique for Human Error Rate Prediction (THERP). Don't be fooled by the title – this research was extremely interesting. Together with current neuroscientific understanding of the human brain, it gives good insight into the mistakes our brain makes.

Knowing such valuable information, by such brilliant minds, was out there drove us to ask new questions. What sort of mistakes do people make? Where inside the brain do we make mistakes? When does the brain realize it has made a mistake? How many mistakes do we make on average, and how can we reduce that number?

Human brains make many different mistakes – some conscious, and some subconscious. We have the ability to detect a consciously made mistake. Most of us have sent an email but forgotten to include the attachment, at least once in our lives. The Journal of Cognitive Neuroscience covers several studies of the 'Anterior Cingulate Cortex' or ACC. This is a fancy scientific term for the 'Oops' center. The ACC plays a key role in detecting mistakes. Research has, however, determined that we do not have an 'Oops' center in our subconscious. Sadly for us, this means that when we make a subconscious mistake, we don't notice. Given the huge amount of decisions that our subconscious is responsible for, it would be extremely handy to have such a center.

The ACC is sensitive to alcohol and drugs. After just a few alcoholic drinks, your ACC goes to sleep and stops functioning. This is the main reason many individuals who have been drinking believe they are still able to drive a car. Some believe they are sharper, have better focus, and are better drivers after a few drinks. Right.

Over time, this has led to the development of all kinds of human error rate tables and techniques. For example:

- Management Oversight Risk Tree (MORT)
- Technique For The Retrospective And Predictive Analysis Of Cognitive Error (TRACEr and TRACEr-lite)
- Technique for Human Error Rate Prediction (THERP)
- Human Error Assessment and Reduction Technique (HEART)
- Human System Interactions (HSYS) (Source Federal Aviation Administration, FAA, USA) and many more

Subconscious mistakes are the most common mistakes made by the brain, and the most dangerous. Over the years, we've drilled down into these techniques, reports and error rate tables. What we've found is intriguing – and scary. Every human with a healthy brain makes, on average, one mistake per hour in the subconscious brain. If we look at this at a corporate level, it means a company with 100 employees produces 4,000 mistakes per week, or 16,000 a month.

We are wasting time. We are forced to spend a considerable quantity of time solving one another's subconsciously made mistakes. Because of this, companies are losing millions of euros/dollars a year. To avoid this kind of damage, management will then try to cut costs, and put a lot of effort and pressure on staff to increase productivity.

The flow-on effect is obvious. Staff become less satisfied, and lose motivation. When people are not happy in their job, their brain registers stress. Stress increases cortisol levels, pushing the number of mistakes even higher.

So we know the pitfalls. How, then, can we reduce the number of subconscious mistakes we make?

To reduce subconsciously made mistakes, we kick off with an examination of key activities. We define key activities as being essential to a single process, and having the highest probability and cost of failure. The analysis we perform is complex, due to a number of factors.

1. Most people view their own job and responsibility as the most important. This is subjective. To identify the real key activities we need an objective set of rules, a proven method, and a brain-friendly management style.
2. It is sometimes difficult to identify a core key activity, because most activities are related. Once identified, it can be a difficult task to estimate the level of risk involved, and to calculate the exact costs of failures made.

Once we identify key activities, we can move on to the next phase – redesigning work processes and developing new protocols. In this phase, our core focus is making the identified activities visible to the conscious brain. We need our conscious brain to pick up these activities, because that's where the ACC lives. Since the ACC operates as our mistake control center, sending these activities there will reduce the number of mistakes we are making.

Truth be told, we cannot avoid all subconscious mistakes. What we can do is catch those subconscious mistakes before they cause problems in our lives.

Let's look at five root causes of mistakes made by the subconscious brain:

1. Automated decisions patterns or biases.
As we've explored, most of our daily decisions are initiated by the subconscious brain. In order to make decisions, the brain uses fixed, or automated, decisions patterns, equal to biases. So far, scientists have documented around 140 to 150 different biases. A famous example is the Door In The Face (DITF) technique, discovered by Cialdini in 1975. First, a large favor is asked. This favor is denied. Then, a smaller favor is asked, which is usually granted. Let's use a quick example to illustrate this technique in action.

A friend approaches you, and says, "Please, can you give me $1,000?" Obviously, you say, "No." Your friend then asks, "Well, can you at least give me $5 then?" We are all more likely to say "Yes" in this scenario, than if the $1,000 request had been left out. If you know how it works, it is not too difficult to fool the brain and influence the outcome of our subconscious decisions.

2. Deformed information.
As pointed out in the law of communication, the brain deforms incoming information to match its archive system. This is one of the main reasons why misinterpretation and wrong assumptions occur.

3. Adjusting memory.
The brain adjusts existing memories, based upon new experiences and information. It does this all without instructing us. As a result we are convinced we know exactly what was said, and what was agreed to, in a situation. In reality, this is not the case.

Many of us go even further, supporting a theory called "counterfactual thinking." Our brain adjusts a memory in order to improve the role we played in a meeting, for example. In that regard, the memory is not reliable or accurate.

4. DNA based discrimination.
Within a fraction of a second, our brain judges the structure of a human face against our pre-programmed interpretation of facial appearance. Our subconscious brain knows, for example, what characteristics belong to a competent face. "Inferences of competence from faces predict Election Outcomes" showed that the outcome of the 2004 election of the senate race was predicted correctly by 68.8 percent of the study's participants.[5] Although the participants selected their candidates willingly, the predictions were made based upon a rational choice. This raises questions, and perhaps serious doubts, around how objective the HR department is in its selection of new candidates.

5. Unreliable short-term memory.
The last reason we need to look at is short-term memory. The short-term memory is exactly that. It only has a capacity of around 60 seconds. Research suggests that, although it might vary from person to person, your short term memory can only hold 4 pieces of new information at the same time. Especially when challenged with an overload of information, the brain loses focus, and overrides the information before it has a chance to be properly stored. This is why so many of us exclaim, "This is important, let me write it down," and then promptly forget about the issue. If you have a point to make, and you want someone to remember it: Limit your input to two or three topics at most. Notice how many politicians do this, the next time you have a chance.

Another element to factor in, when it comes to our unreliable brain, is that it lies often. That may not come as a surprise to you. Some scientists claim that an adult lies three times in every ten minute period. We not only lie to others; we also lie to ourselves. If you want to delve deeper into why we lie so much, or how to stop, we'll leave that to experts like Dan Ariely. For the purposes of this book, all we need to know is that our brain is lying to us, and to others. A lot.

With this in mind, and armed with the five root causes of subconscious mistakes, it is advisable not to take yourself too seriously. Try and keep your newfound brain knowledge in mind, and think twice before you start a discussion with, "I absolutely know for sure…"

Given these unavoidable failures of the brain, it is much smarter to build a management team who expect these consistent shortcomings. Create a smart team which uses these considerations, instead of battling against them.

Error management

We have reviewed most of the imperfections of our brain. Making mistakes, forgetting, and lying are all a part of being human, and have no bearing on our intelligence. Making mistakes is an unpleasant fact of life.

It is much wiser to consider these new and unpleasant discoveries in relation to how we deal with mistakes, and how we relate to the people who make them. When we optimize an organization, we construct a culture that permits making mistakes. Only by admitting mistakes can a company achieve high performance excellence. We advise top-level executives and entrepreneurs to design an organization that can detect mistakes faster. As in all areas of life, if we can see the mistake, we can move to solve it instantly.

To achieve those kinds of results, we need to rearrange work processes. An important factor, which we encourage in managers, is to compliment individuals when they detect and resolve a mistake.

By using this indirect approach, management creates an environment where people produce positive hormones, instead of stress hormones due to making mistakes. An additional effect is that positive hormones reduce the likelihood of mistakes, whereas stress hormones increase their probability.

There are some departments, industries, or jobs where mistakes need to be completely eliminated. Nuclear power plants, as an example, or in aviation, or in our world's hospitals. In those cases, we create different protocols to bring the most important steps of every process from the subconscious to the conscious.

Success management

Success management creates great results, if we apply it correctly. An example of good application is using someone's individual success to correct the group's direction. In this way, we can indirectly correct the individuals who made a mistake.

Let's say that you are the chairman of a meeting. Person "A" performed well, and person "C" did not perform so well. In applying the law of Success Management, you would compliment person "A," and invite her to explain to the group the key factors to her success. Person "C" will realize his underperformance, without you having to explain to him where he went wrong. Person "C" is smart enough to filter the information shared by person "A," and will use the right elements to emulate that success next time.

In addition, your sincere compliment triggers person "A" to produce positive hormones, which prompts the other team members in a positive way. As we now know, happy hormones diminish mistakes.

Brain laws necessary for every method

There is an inexhaustible number of management books. This, on top of literature about business models like LEAN, Operational Excellence, Blue Ocean, Business Model Generation, Total Quality Management, High Performance Organization, and so on. What they all have in common is they promise a flawless organization, decreased costs and increased sales. The hidden venom lies in the acceptance, implementation, and securing of the suggested changes. Independent from the chosen method, the human brain resists general changes. To achieve the desired outcome and a long lasting result, one needs an advanced knowledge of how the brain functions. After that, we're still faced with how the brain laws are applied.

With the preceding six brain laws; intrinsic motivation, self-determination, relevance, communication, healthy time balance and success management, you're armed with all the fundamental tools. However, there is one crucial element missing.

Humans are creatures of habit. To make sure that we can establish general changes successfully, we need to gather a few more ingredients over the next three chapters.

17. The brain knowledge vault

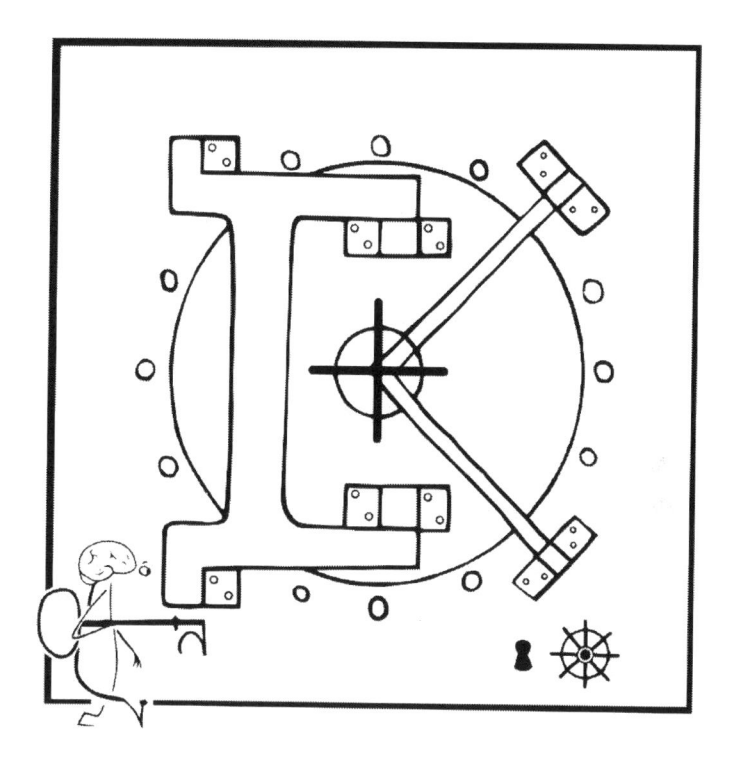

Brainer 17

If we put information in a vault, it can't get out. We cannot reach into that vault if we do not have the right key, or the right combination, or the right PIN number. This is, and has been, the challenge facing neuroscientists for many years, in their attempt to figure out the real workings of our brain.

Thanks to the fMRI scanner and EEG, we have discovered a lot about our brain over the last twenty-five years. By understanding the basic systems the brain uses for recording and processing data, we can make use of that new knowledge in our daily lives.

As our knowledge grows, the demand for new systems and ways of applying it on a daily scale grows, too. This knowledge is what drove us to create around 200 brain laws. Now that we've shared our crucial driving brain laws with you, it becomes much easier to recognize and learn the standard processes and steps the brain is following.

If only it was that simple. Our brains have a functional design that does not differ from one to the next, generally speaking. Still, our DNA, combined with the programming in our early years, makes each of us a unique individual. With the use of the brain laws, we can create sources of recognition, like touchstones for your brain. We can help our brain to appreciate why it does what it does best. Why does it guard its secrets so carefully? Why won't it open? These questions barely break the surface of the subconscious vault.

It is mind blowing to discover how this subconscious part of the brain makes decisions, how it rules feelings, and how it becomes the winner over ratio most of the time. Where is our knowledge stored away in the brain?

The quickest, least helpful answer is: somewhere and anywhere, at the same time. Research shows that our brain doesn't operate like a computer. It doesn't operate like books on a bookshelf. It is not a file cabinet, where exact information is stored and retrieved later on. If we describe knowledge as memories, we then have a few types of memory. For the purposes of this book, we're going to discuss two types.

The first is procedural memory, which is the learning and execution of skills. The second is declarative memory, which we can break down even further, into two parts.

Part one is the episodic memory that stores situations or events that have happened in the past. Part two is the factual memory that stores information or facts.

On a neurobiological level, this implies that our brain stores information as millions of rapid changes between neurons. These changes occur at the connection points – the synapses. In these neural networks, we can find a close alliance between certain neurons to create, store, and retrieve a certain memory. The brain decides the importance of storage, based on value or repetition. If we repeat something more often, the brain will decide that it is more important than information not repeated at all.

This is how we learn to play a musical instrument, for example. Repetition will activate many standalone parts of the brain and body at the same time. When playing an instrument, the brain needs to create hand/hand, ear, eye, short- and long-term storage capacity in the brain, all at the same time. As we've learned, the brain is not a great multitasker, and so these processes are executed in queue within milliseconds. This gives the impression that we are multitasking.

At a recent seminar, someone asked, "Will our brain ever run out of memory?" Our brain's retention is low, unless someone is an autistic savant. Some savants come to an incredible level of 95 percent retention. This means, of course, that the answer is "No." It is rather safe to say our brain will never run out of memory in our lifetime. If the brain registers that it needs more memory, it could do three things:

1. Grow more brain cells, which would be evolutionary process that could take thousands of years.
2. Forget old memories that have no purpose in today's existence. The brain would then free up memory space to store current events, and retrieve them later as needed.

3. Create additional, new, smarter neural connections and networks. As we speak, your brain already has trillions of these. If we compare the size of our skull to that of the Neanderthal, it is surprising to see that our skull is one and a half times smaller, but houses greater capacity and intelligence.

Even with these options at our brain's disposal, it is already prioritizing all its new and old information. It is deciding whether the information is needed today, or in the near or far future.

18. Never be the same

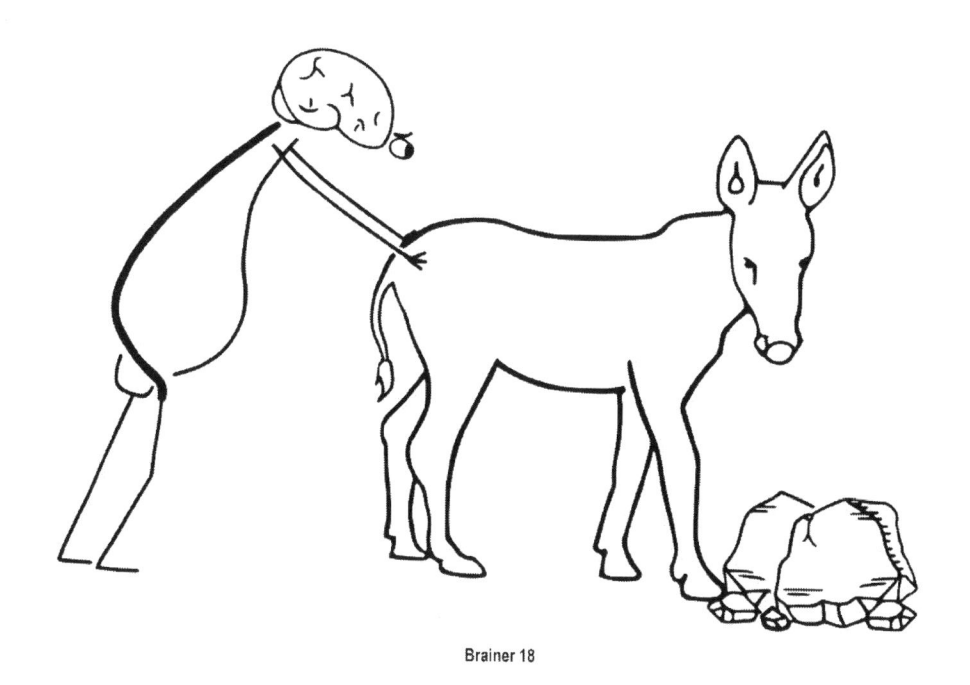

Brainer 18

I cannot be with him because he is such a difficult person. How many times have you found yourself in this situation? The question we have to ponder here is: why do we think of someone as a difficult person? If we're honest with ourselves, it is usually because that person does not agree with us, thinks differently to us, or is driven by different motives. We can also state that their archive system is filled with different experiences, opinions and rule sets. The subconscious brain sees this other opinion or behavior as a threat.

Now that we are aware of how our brain functions, and we are armed with our new brain laws, we can search for advantages. Our filter system limits our views because it functions like a membrane.

All our incoming and outgoing information is modified in such a way that it cannot pass through the membrane. This, as we've explored, is why our brain is not capable of receiving all the opportunities that are offered to us. Living and working with people who have a different membrane will expand our opportunities and chances for success. This is how excellent teams are put together.

We've learned that our brain is deceiving us 800 to 1,000 times a day. This is freeing information. It means we do not have to take ourselves too serious any longer. We are familiar with how our brain adjusts our original experience, and how it alters our memories. Maybe the most remarkable fact is that our opinions, convictions and positions are not even our own. We are carrying opinions that have been projected upon us by others. When we try to come up with a reason to explain why we have made a certain decision, we now realize our ratio is just inventing reasons to justify our subconscious decision. We also recognize that our subconscious brain possesses an unreliable subset of rules and biases, which it is using to carry out at least 95 percent of our daily decisions.

This is starting to sound scary – maybe even discouraging. Fear not. The good news is that when our conscious knows how the subconscious works, it cannot be fooled so easily anymore. We have discovered how to bring important decisions from the subconscious to the intelligent part of our brain. We have determined that we should pay attention to what we want to do, and who we want to be, as a human being.

Learning and unlearning

So now we face a new question: how are we going to apply all this new knowledge in real life? That's the goal, isn't it? We need some tricks, so we can learn more quickly and effectively. We want to boost our brainpower. Our brain has a specific instruction – a method of learning – that works best for us. Once we comprehend how it works, learning becomes infinitely easier.

It is our experience that traditional learning methods do not work well in real life. Research shows that we forget 80 percent of what we learn, within two or three weeks. We need to change this, but how? We discussed this topic with behavior specialists and neuroscientists. Without exception, they all determined that the effectiveness of training, education and learning all come down to one simple factor: does our brain think the information is relevant, or not?

Our brain's neuroplasticity is huge – everyone has the capacity for learning. That is not the problem. One interesting challenge we face, however, is our archive system. Information stored in the archive system is the brain's truth. Existing information prevails over new information. The brain logic behind this is that new information needs to prove its trustworthiness, because the brain wants to avoid pain and gain happiness. The older we get, the more our archive system is filled. Therefore, it is harder for older people to adapt to new information. Fortunately for us, when the archive system is blank on a certain topic, the brain has fewer problems adopting information relating to it.

Existing knowledge already contains its own "highway" systems, and is more valuable than new information, at first. The brain will always take these existing highways, as long as there is no alternative path. The brain does not care whether the highway leads to the desired result or not.

We all know people in our network who are successful in failure. Their brain is reliable in processing the information, but the highway just doesn't lead to the result they want.

We need to understand that the brain cannot unlearn until it has learned something new. The brain cannot take another highway if one does not exist. If our brain registers something new as relevant it will create a new, small neural connection. Sticking with our highway analogy, this small neural connection would be a dirt road. When this dirt road leads to a desired outcome, the brain upgrades it to a two-lane sealed road. After many repetitions, the brain finally converts the sealed road to a new highway. Depending on how often we use the new dirt road, it takes the brain anywhere from 30 to 90 days to transform it into a highway. From a biological and evolutionary point of view, this is fast.

Companies have methods of testing their personnel. These are commonly called evaluations, and they are enough to put most brains into a state of fear. During an evaluation, the boss, manager, or leader will identify and discuss areas of improvement with an employee.

The outcome might see the employee attending training courses or seminars, to improve their skills. Many employees will even thank their boss for giving them the opportunity to improve their skills.

Here are where the wheels fall off. In most cases, there is an important correlation between the subjects we do not like, and actions we are not executing well. Trying to teach someone something that he does not like is, most often, senseless. It is why so many training and development programs are unproductive from the start.

19. How to apply in actual practice

Brainer 19

The usual remarks and questions we receive after trainings, seminars, and master classes with top executives follow one line of thinking. Recently, one of our executives approached us, explaining, "Gents, I have been around for many years and I convinced myself I knew it all, but what you people have taught me today is next level personal growth. This was really, really, really, interesting. I finally realize that I know absolutely nothing about the functioning of my own brain. Yet I rely on my brain making the right decisions every second of the day. As you guys have stated….it is not my fault… I'm just following the white rabbit.

Now I have your information, and I do not want to go back to where I was. I need to have this information available to learn how to apply this in my everyday life. Can you give me a guideline to train my brain daily, within the possibilities of the neuroplasticity mentioned?"

We understand the importance of a simple directional scheme. We knew we had to create one, for you to better understand what your brain does in autonomous mode. To capitalize on the changes happening for you right now, we will follow this up with a step-by-step plan for you to follow, and a way to test and recognize your personal growth.

Bear in mind that a healthy brain needs around 30 to 90 days to create new neural connections to replace the old ones. <u>At the end of the book we have created some exercises</u>. These exercises will kick start your personal disruption, and move you towards the activation of your intrinsic motivation. This is the map to becoming a better 'YOU'.

We divide the standard working process of the brain into 3 segments:

1. To recognize and research
2. To acknowledge and accept
3. To conclude and apply

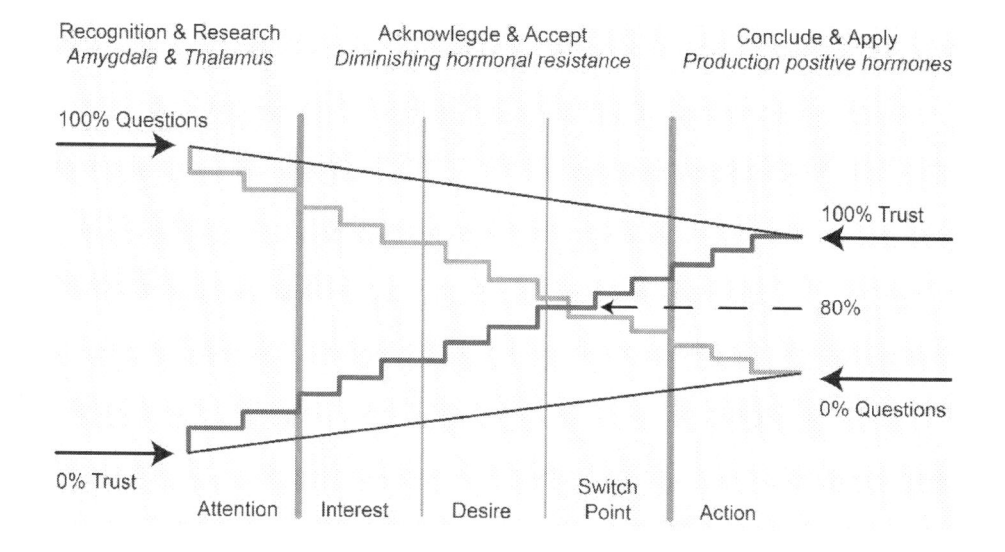

```
Recognition & Research        Acknowlegde & Accept              Conclude & Apply
Amygdala & Thalamus      Diminishing hormonal resistance    Production positive hormones
```

```
100% Questions                                                    100% Trust

                                                                  80%

                                                                  0% Questions
0% Trust
         Attention  | Interest | Desire | Switch  | Action
                                         Point
```

Our brain can handle what is going on here in around 250 milliseconds, and operates in this mode 24/7.

Step 1. To recognize and research

By now, you've accepted that the primary resistance of your brain is extremely strong, and is encouraged by your fear system. When it comes to changes, the fear system will force you towards the "Yes, but if..." questions. Alternatively, it might be driving you down the "Well, I don't believe..." route. This is a completely normal process. It is your brain's way of trying to hold on to what it believes it knows. It is important to start this process of change in a brain-friendly way. The first step is to realize that what you have read in this book is just another truth. Another created truth, aside from yours. You and your educators not only created your truth, but also pre-programmed your brain to believe that it is the only truth. This results in thick neural connections that do not want to separated.

Your brain is now formulating a queue of biological steps, which it is planning to execute in quick succession. It will start by questioning 100 percent of this new information, whilst having zero percent trust. We're going to embrace this as the basic and normal process that occurs when it comes in contact with other truths. Your brain is attempting to prove its own right, and to hold on to its own truth, created in the past.

When the new information we are presenting piques your brain's interest, your brain will refer back to this book and do research. When your research leads to recognition, your brain will register this new information as relevant. Gradually, as answers are accepted by your brain, the questions will diminish, and trust will grow. As part of your brain's recognition and research phase, you can refer to the above illustration.

Step 2. To acknowledge and accept

As we arrive at step 2, the primary resistance is still there, but at a lower level. The subconscious brain is alert, but will allow enough room to acknowledge that it might be possible that this new truth can help to create a better version of you. Our experience is that during steps 1 and 2, the people we mentor have many questions. They also become explicitly honest about who they are, how they feel and respond to situations, other people, their work environment, and more. It seems that the brain finds pleasure in being honest about what you have become, in search of new findings.

This is a crucial step towards acceptance. During this part of the process, the people we mentor start investigating; reading books, watching videos on the internet, gaining general knowledge on the subject at hand.

They develop a craving for information on the more technical aspects of the workings of their brain. They want to know how the brain engine actually operates, and how to use this new knowledge on a daily basis.

The brain realizes that, from an evolutionary point of view, it needs to know more about its functioning. As you can see in the illustration, it isn't until we reach 80 percent questioning that the brain is ready, willing and able to widen and enhance the thin neural connections into thicker neural connections. This point, where the two green lines intersect with each other in the illustration, is our "switch point." Now the brain is ready to step into the next phase.

Step 3. To conclude and apply

When your brain accepts that this is a better way to create the advanced version of yourself, it will relentlessly push forward to learn how to apply the new findings in real life. This is your intrinsic motivation. Some people call it passion, or endless drive.

At this point, your brain can become almost religious about the new findings, wanting to share them with whoever gives an indication they see a change in you or your behavior. Your brain is excited by questions like, "Why are you looking so happy lately?" People who are not in balance instantly sense a level of balance in others. Do not underestimate the power of the sensory emotional brain to identify balance in somebody else. This is just another phenomenal capability of your brain.

When humans find inner balance between subconscious and conscious, we produce a mixture of positive hormones. The combination of our adjusted behavior and a surplus of dopamine, oxytocin and serotonin floating freely through our brain and body send signals to others – something has changed in you.

We prepare the people we mentor to recognize the impact of these 3 steps. Because we have been doing this for so many years, we can predict the outcome of our sessions for each individual. This is all part of why we love what we do. We activate the intrinsic motivational system in humans, empowering them to become happier than they have ever been. We are successful in doing what we love to do, just by teaching the brain how it functions.

By simply teaching your brain to listen to its internal biological and chemical processes, we are helping it get its internal direction back. Throughout this journey, your brain becomes a better leader over these biological and chemical processes. It restores inner balance, culminating in happiness and better health.

This was no accident, for us. We were driven to discover the *cause* of our feelings, intellect and behavior, and to explore all the functions of the human brain, for this exact reason. Focusing on the effects – the symptoms – felt like we were missing something monumental. Besides, there are plenty of people already doing that on our little blue planet. We humans needed something new.

Based upon what we've spent years learning and sharing, we have developed the **Neural Cause Effect** (NCE) method. We apply the NCE method to teach decision makers our step-by-step framework for solving discrepancies between cause and effect.

You don't need to have built a house to know you need a solid foundation. Without a solid foundation, you cannot build a solid house. The same applies to our brain.

The NCE method focuses on building this foundation for our brain. This foundation is essential to recalibrating existing actions, habits, opinions, and beliefs.

To do this, we need to remember what we've learned: it is fundamentally impossible for the brain to first unlearn old, hard-coded actions, habits, opinions, or beliefs.

To make a change, the brain needs to build new neural networks before the existing old neural networks become inactive. In this context, the brain laws of intrinsic motivation, self-determination and relevance play an important role.

20. Conclusion

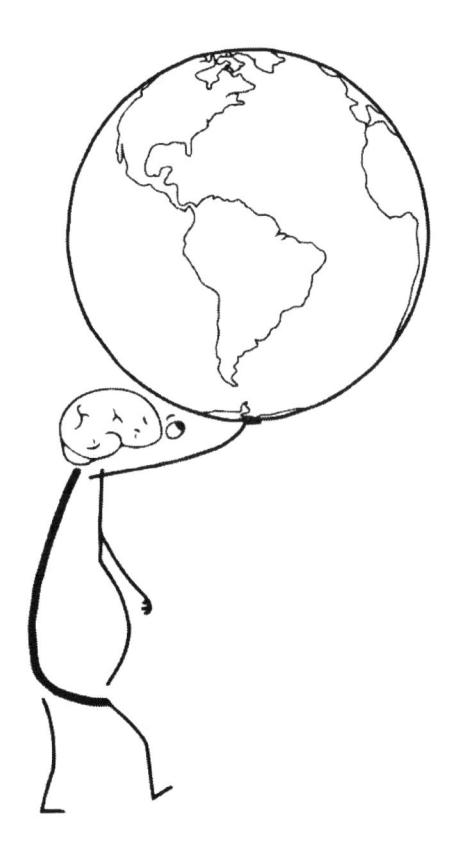

Brainer 20

Here is something we learned while we spent two years writing this book: we need new leaders in this world. Leaders who are able to create and maintain a new style of leadership. Leadership that lifts our society into a new knowledge-based era. The leaders we have in mind are not an existential ideal; we mean YOU. You, as an individual, being responsible for your personal microenvironment in this world.

When you can improve your microenvironment, it will branch out in a positive way and affect the microenvironments around you. This will become positively contagious, and show a better course of human progress on a global level.

SparkWise Quote:
"Balanced teams create departments, cooperative departments create an organization, and a cooperative organization is a company."

Before we started on our own journey of discovery, we approached our mentorship differently. When we helped organizations to improve, our starting point was always: Mission, Vision, and Strategy. After that, we would work from the top down, right through the organizational layers to improve departments, teams, individuals, software, hardware, suppliers and clients.

Now, with the added value of human DNA and neuroscientific knowledge, we have changed that model. We are still loyal to Mission, Vision, and Strategy. That has to be clear on all levels of the organization. Not only clear, but it also has to be within the social DNA of the employees of the company, so to speak.

But, since 2012 we have been building from the bottom up. We turned the model on its head. After defining our methods to investors, owners, shareholders and Management, we are given Carte Blanche to implement our methods.

Within the organization, we always start with the individuals. All you need are two individuals to create a team. If your two team members do not understand the workings of their own brain, how will they ever understand each other? We've already learned that misunderstanding builds conflicts. The flipside to this coin is that understanding creates balance. With this new biological DNA- and neuroscientific-driven method, we are capable of changing the face of success. To count, we have successfully improved 350 SME and Corporate companies in Europe. These organizations are home to between 100 and 30,000 full-time equivalent (fte) employees. Big or small, the basics remain the same: work bottom up instead of top down; teach the individuals how their brains operate. Create common ground for coworkers that have gained the same knowledge. The buzz on the work floor after a training session creates perception of behavioral structures, moods and responses.

The advantage of the SparkWise method, as it has evolved over the years, is that it embraces brain-friendly communication. This results in more empathy among employees. Less conflict on the work floor, less stress, and therefore no excessive cortisol increase. A structural decline of cortisol production opens the door for our happiness hormones to circulate through our system.

Dopamine and oxytocin makes people excited and, most of all, friendly. This drives improved productivity, less sick leave, higher output, greater profits, and a stronger emotional engagement with a brand people want to work for.

As we all know, the people in our workforce are our intrinsic capital. Nowadays, that is more valid than ever. Through social media, whether you like it or not, people will talk about where they work. They will reveal how their superiors, management, and colleagues treat them. This can damage the core of your brand. Most organizations discover this damage way too late, when it has seeped into the bottom line. We also know that Profit and Loss reports and accounting figures are a way of looking to the past, trying to predict the future. Today it is imperative to use the right tools to respond to what is taking place in the market right now. Many big brands have destroyed their markets by clinging to old school ways and directive leadership. They are, effectively, steering from their ivory towers, too far away from the actual market to see where they're heading.

Now, your market is no longer just your clients. An essential part of your market is your workforce; these are the people talking to your existing and future clients and competitors every day. An unhappy workforce will create unhappy clients. Unhappy clients will move away from stressful people, burning your brand in the process. Unhappy clients can express their displeasure on social media, and reach millions of people within seconds. This snowball effect is so powerful, in fact, that major established companies, built up over decades, can be wiped out within a few years.

We are one of the few teams in the world that have created a liquid improvement system to ensure gains of $1,000,000 net profit per 200 fte employees. By starting with supporting intrinsic human capital, we create a happy workforce. They will fulfil their regular tasks because they like what they do.

Through this process, they become ambassadors and informal leaders on the work floor. Why do we need to share this with you?

Let's look at some scary numbers for a minute. Replacing an employee costs, on average, 150 percent of their annual salary. This entails loss of education, and loss of intellectual knowledge, as well as the time cost of sourcing, recruiting, and onboarding their replacement. Smart companies that have embraced the current market, instead of remaining in the past, know that preventive measures are cheaper than resolving problems later.

What we want to say is this: humans are the most important factor in these fast changing markets. We are confident that throughout your journey with us here, you've gained that valuable insight, too.

Quality employee education is a relatively small investment. How it builds new leadership and brand ambassadors is an exponential return on that investment. Empowering your workforce will elevate an organization in the most rewarding ways.

We are also confident that our SparkWise vision – your new knowledge of biological DNA and neuroscientific insights – will shed new light on what you are doing today.

As we leave you with the learning materials that will help your new journey of discovery and, ultimately, success, we'd like to thank you. It has been a pleasure to share our discoveries, hypotheses, philosophies and four decades of practical knowledge with you. We are excited to hear your thoughts on the subjects we've shared here.

We want you to meet others like you; curious, driven individuals with a drive to achieve great things. You can talk amongst yourselves, and be each other's sounding boards, by registering on our private. Facebook page.

We know some of you will like our information, and others will not. We'd like to challenge you, in your discussions with each other, to search for <u>similarities</u> instead of <u>differences</u>. What an excellent learning opportunity this could be. Challenge your brain to do so from a conscious standpoint, instead of letting your subconscious take the reins. It is not an easy thing for us to do. When we make an effort to bring our standpoint from the subconscious to the conscious, we are actually already getting into the new SparkWise way. We hope you will see this as one of the many ways you are growing in this new method.

We hope you have fun identifying all these processes within yourself and others. Please take advantage of the following exercise book, to start developing your new neural networks and sharing the experience with your friends, colleagues, and (social) networks.

SparkWise Quote:
"Humanity lacks general brain knowledge. Only by improving individual brain knowledge, can humans transform – becoming balanced and more successful"

21. Summary

We do not like summaries. We do not like summaries because we prefer to condense summary information into two sentences. So, here are our two sentences:

"Most people focus on the effects instead of the cause."

And:

"The cause is a lack of knowledge of our brain. If that is not clear by now, please read the book again...:)"

SPARKWISE

Exercise Book

'Why' of Everything

"Why of Everything" is not about personal development.
It is about personal disruption.
Without personal disruption, personal growth is virtually impossible.

This SparkWise guide can show you how to harness the latest brain knowledge in your professional and personal life – every day.

Part 2

22. Exercise Book: Why of Everything

How can we realize the start of our neural network change in only 14 days?

Brainer 21

An important element of the SparkWise hypothesis is to teach the brain how the brain functions. It is important to exercise and experience, for yourself, how to stimulate your brain to develop into this new direction.

The effectiveness of this element rests in its simplicity and universal applicability. Being told the why and how of other people's success will not help you, as a unique individual, at all.

What helps YOU is teaching your own brain the essence of how it functions. You have read this book. You've received the basic ingredients to activate your personal development. The next step is to put the new knowledge to the test. As you start these exercises, we're reprogramming your brain, step-by-step.

You know now that the brain is capable of massive change, thanks to neuroplasticity. We're not here to lie to you – this process is 30 to 90 days of challenging work. The results grow moderately. But if we look at those 90 days in context, your brain has taken maybe 30 to 50 years to build up certain convictions and habits. It is unrealistic to expect instant change. As you move through this process, though, you'll realize that 90 days pass by in the blink of an eye, whether you are creating massive life changes, or staying where you were.

A quick tip before we get started on our exercises: your subconscious brain will put up serious resistance before it lets go of your old habits and convictions.

We want to support you in realizing your dream. We have developed exercises to help you grow new neural networks. All of the exercises operate in close relation to each other. As you go along you will grow new neural networks, but only if your brain decides the exercise and information presented is relevant. Being consistent, and working through this plan for the next two weeks, establishes your strong foundation. With that foundation, your brain retains the right ingredients for success.

Finally, we'd like to hear your individual results.

Please share your experiences on our Facebook page so that other people can celebrate with you and new conversations can start.

Another quick tip: Most people use a dedicated notebook or take notes in their phone, to write or record their answers.

The following chapters A to S are related to each previous chapter number 1 to 19 in the same order.

A. Have you ever wondered?

How do you question life? What is your personal quest? What is essential to you? Success is different to everyone. To become successful, you need to know and understand your own definition of success. Answer the following 5 questions. It is also helpful to revisit, and comment on, your answers after your first week of this process.

1. What is your definition of success?

$$$$

2. If anything was possible, what would you want to achieve in life? Answer this question like there are no limitations–no "buts" or "ifs."

$$$$

3. What is your deadline for accomplishing your goals? Remember that the brain overestimates what you can do in a year, but underestimates what you can do in three years.

4. What elements do you require to achieve your goal?

5. What kind of people do you need to surround yourself with, to achieve your goal?

B. Biological DNA related to passion

To know your true passion is essential. DNA is the instigator of true passion and shapes that feeling in your subconscious. This is why we physically feel passion.

In our society, it is difficult to pay attention to our feelings and passions. Even so, it is important to realize that your passion lives in your subconscious. To set up a clear view of how your passion is established, we can create a *top ten* list of activities you enjoy, and a *bottom ten* list of activities you dislike.

	Activities I dislike	Activities I enjoy
1		
2		
3		
4		
5		
6		
7		
8		
9		
10		

C. Brain school and brain knowledge

Fighting symptoms – consequences – occupies the minds of 7 and a half billion people, every day. That many people on our little blue planet don't know how to identify and solve the root of their problems. When you struggle to achieve your goals, there is a high chance that you are fighting symptoms as well. The next three questions can help you to get a better understanding of *cause* in your life.

Answer the following three questions:

1. What, to you, are your five biggest failures in life? Now that you know more about how your brain functions, what do you think these failures stemmed from? This is the cause. The cause lies in WHY you feel, behave, and act as you do. Knowing what you know now about how your past programs your beliefs and convictions, would you act differently?

2. What, to you, are your five biggest successes in life? Again, knowing what you do about your brain's functionality, what did your successes stem from? Why were you successful in this area? Which of the brain laws supported your success? More than this, what do you need to do to reproduce your successes?

3. What keeps you from achieving the goals you wrote down in section A?

D. Our perceptive truth versus the fMRI scanner

It's time to explore another question: does one overall truth exist? Even our own truth is a perceptive truth. Our perceptive truth is a product of our DNA, upbringing and later registrations.

Truth is not an intangible thought, just randomly floating around in our brain. It is certain chemicals, inside a set of neural connections, transported by electrical signals. When you change the chemicals or change the connections, you will change your truth.

Using the table below, you can make a list of the behaviors, convictions and rules you need to change, to achieve your goals faster.

	Existing behavior, convictions, set of rules which do not contribute to your success	What problems do they cause YOU?
1		
2		
3		
4		
5		
6		
7		
8		
9		
10		

E. Primitive natural resistance

The non-intelligent part of your brain does not want to change. The brain comes up with many self-invented non-arguments. How can you detect whether those arguments are true, or are misleading you to stop you from making a change in your life?

In the previous exercise, you listed the behaviors, convictions, and rules which prevent you from achieving your goals. For each of those listed convictions answer the next three questions:

1. Is this behavior, conviction, set of rules your own, or is it something ingrained through your upbringing?

2. What would go wrong if you let go of your current behavior, conviction or set of rules? Is your current mindset a fact, or an assumption? When it is an assumption, can you trust it?

3. What facts do you need to have, to establish whether a behavior, conviction, or set of rules is rational or emotional?

F. The hormone factory

Hormones determine how you feel. How you feel has an impact on how you think and behave. You can steer the production of positive hormones. More positive hormones racing around inside our brain and body will lead to better decisions and a better life.

Before you go to sleep, write your achievements for the day in your notebook, or on your phone. Count your blessings. After writing your achievements and blessings, read those of the previous three days.

When you wake up, read those again. We want you to commit to this daily routine for at least the next four weeks. We promise: you'll feel infinitely better for it.

G. The triune brain theory of dr. Paul MacLean

So, we've realized that our subconscious brain is 'boss,' and is making most of our decisions, most of the time. This is unfortunate. More unfortunate still is the unreliable archive system our subconscious is basing its decision-making on. Most of the time this is not a problem, but in certain circumstances, it can be a massive problem. We need to train the brain to detect misleading decisions.

Exercise:

Make a list of at least three important decisions you have made in the last week. For each of those decisions, we have a challenge for you. Imagine that you are going to earn $100,000 to find enough arguments and facts to prove why your decision was wrong (Disclaimer: we aren't actually giving you $100,000. Sorry.)

By doing this challenge you are forcing the ratio to reason, to think practically, and you are giving the subconscious brain less chance to interfere with the decision-making process.

1.

2.

3.

H. A healthy brain

A healthy brain is essential in becoming successful and maintaining that success. We developed a checklist for you.

	Healthy brain habits	✓	Unhealthy brain habits	✗
1	Passion for your work		Drugs and alcohol	
2	Keep your promises		Nicotine and caffeine	
3	Steer production of positive hormones		Granulated or refined sugar consumption	
4	Healthy diet		Diabetes	
5	Healthy weight		Obesity	
6	Nutrition for the brain		High blood pressure	

	Healthy brain habits	✓	**Unhealthy brain habits**	✗
7	Stress management		Chronic stress	
8	Brain exercises		Important decisions based on emotion	
9	Learn and master new information /habits		Activities or sports which damage the brain	
10	Exercise daily		Less than 45 minutes of exercise a day	
11	Clean environment		Peer group with unhealthy habits	
12	Up to 7 – 8 hours sleep		Insomnia	

If you can check off eight of the 12 healthy brain habits, you stand at the healthy end of the scale. If you can check off more than four of the 12 unhealthy brain habits, reconsider your lifestyle.

I. The eighth noteworthy brain parts

When we take care of our brain, our brain will take care of us. The next 5 ingredients add to the quality of your life.

1. Drink between 2 and 2.5 liters of water throughout the day. Herbal tea counts as water ↓ coffee does not. It can be better for your body to take small sips of water every few minutes, rather than guzzling full glasses at once. The most important thing is to stay hydrated. If you feel thirsty, you are already too late.
2. Eat food with a healthy cholesterol balance. Avocado, salmon, herring, mackerel, coconut oil, walnuts, are all healthy cholesterol choices. A dietician can help you to put a plan together. Or, like most of us, you can Google it.
3. Add blue and red fruits ↓ blueberries, strawberries, raspberries, pomegranate, and so on ↓ to your daily diet.
4. Make sure you move for 30 to 45 minutes every day. Walking, taking the stairs instead of the elevator, bicycling, or swimming, is enough. You do not have to work out extensively in the gym.
5. Reduce the intake of granulated and refined sugars as much as possible.

J. Brain laws revealed

As you probably know by now, the brain works in a specific order. To unlearn, we first have to create new neural connections. In sections D and E, you wrote down the behaviors, convictions, and set of rules you wish to change.

Exercise:

Describe the new set of behaviors, convictions and set of rules which will replace the old ones. We've created a table for you below, to help you work through this step.

	New behavior, convictions, set of rules	How do these contribute to your success?
1		
2		
3		
4		
5		
6		
7		
8		
9		
10		

K. The law of intrinsic motivation

The correlation between strong neural connections and intrinsic motivation is crystal clear. When repeating all your exercises every day, change will happen faster than you could expect.

Exercise:

Use the same five components of chapter 11 to activate your individual intrinsic motivation. Use "leading by asking" to create a counter question. For example, when you feel negative in any situation, ask yourself out loud: what elements do I need to become positive?

Working this way and thinking out of the box will support the activation of your new behaviors, convictions and set of rules.

L. The law of self determination

Ignoring self-determination has a negative impact on intrinsic motivation. It is important to train the brain to recognize when others ignore your self-determination. This exercise registers how many times a day that happens to you.

Exercise:

Keep a specific daily log of how many times your self-determination is violated by others, and how often you violate the self-determination of others.

M. The law of relevance

To program your relevance detection system, we've got two techniques you can apply throughout your journey. Programming your relevance detection system creates new neural connections for your new behaviors, convictions and set of rules. As a result, they will grow faster and stronger. This helps you to enable faster change.

Exercise:

Create a mood board to visualize your goals. Use pictures and text. Copy the mood board and place copies in different locations. At home, in the office, in your car, on your computer, on your telephone – you want to see it several times a day. Develop a clear, personal motto of what you want to achieve.

Your motto has to work for you, but we can give you a couple of examples that people share with us:

"I KNOW I can create a better version of myself and achieve my goals."

"I need to train my brain how my brain operates."

Set the alarm on your mobile for eight times a day. As soon as the alarm goes off, repeat your motto out loud for one minute. This might sound weird, but your brain needs repetition, repetition, and more repetition to accept a change. Just thinking about it rationally is not enough for your brain to accept and effect change.

N. The law of communication

Brain-friendly communication is important for several reasons. Firstly, people behave in a more constructive way when we communicate in a brain-friendly way. Working in social harmony becomes easier. It helps us to achieve our goals. To make brain-friendly communication second nature, we deliver 8 different techniques in chapter 14. Do you remember them? If not, feel free to go back for a refresher course. If your recall is stronger already, let's get started.

To master these techniques, we need to practice and review our behaviors.

Exercise:

Take a moment in the middle of each day to run through your discussions this morning. Check what went well and what did not. Review whether you applied the 8 guidelines of brain-friendly communication.

O. The law of healthy time balance

To keep our intrinsic motivation activated, we need to spend around 50 percent of our time on activities we love.

Exercise:

Visit our healthy time balance page on our website and use the Healthy Time Balance form.
(http://www.whyofeverything.com/healthytimebalance)

Use our formula to calculate the health of your time balance. Establish what actions you have to take to achieve a healthy time balance, and how you are going to execute those.

P. Success management based on neuroscience

Success management is the conductor of the five other brain laws: *intrinsic motivation*, *self-determination*, *relevance*, *communication* and healthy *time balance*.

When you are consistently executing all exercises, you are building strong experience and application of the five brain laws. This measure of experience is crucial in propelling you to the next level. By sharing your brain knowledge with others, you can really extend your personal experience.

We encourage participants of our advanced personal mentoring program to choose a trusted mentee. The responsibility of the participator is to lead the mentee through the steps of success you have access to in this book. The reason why becoming a mentor is so valuable is simple. Mastering brain laws, to the point where you can share them with others in a valuable way, takes a lot of practice and repetition.

Exercise:

Find a mentee, and share what you have learned in this book. Each week, tune into how your mentee responds to the information you share, on a subconscious and conscious level. The advantage of sharing your findings as a mentor, is that your subconscious brain needs to be creative in searching for answers and conclusions to the questions your mentee comes up with. A mentor/mentee relationship keeps you both on your toes. As a result, the subconscious brain learns to trust the conscious brain, which will create inner balance.

The effect of helping someone else on their own journey of growth is priceless. It contributes to your self-esteem and makes this world a better place. That makes you feel valued and important!

Q. The brain knowledge vault

One of the most challenging processes in personal development is to get your conscious brain in balance with your subconscious brain. The subconscious brain does not give up its dominance easily. It will use tricks and lies to hold onto its control. It is important to be clued-up to this phenomenon, and to recognize the evasive attempts of your subconscious.

Negative thoughts are not *just happening*, your hormones are driving them. We must recognize a sudden or slow building negative thought as an attempt of the subconscious brain to keep control. The subconscious brain is using its pre-programmed archive to produce the hormones that trigger feelings of negativity and uncertainty. It is possible to reverse negative thoughts in a few ways, and we need to do it fast.

Exercise:

1. Go outside and walk it off. Fifteen to twenty minutes is enough.

2. Read your happy notes and blessings, and repeat them out loud.

3. Think of your successes in life, in such a way that you can feel the joy and pride again.

4. Write the negative thought you feel. By writing the negative thought, you exchange the negative thought from subconscious to conscious. This way, the conscious brain can fight the feeling.

5. Write down all the way in which your negative thought or feeling is wrong. Do not accept the feeling. Take control back over this feeling.

R. Never be the same

During an average day, a lot happens. We attend meetings; we receive messages and mails; we meet and talk to people, we listen, we argue – although much less than we used to–, we laugh, and so on. Our subconscious brain labels every event as positive, negative, or neutral. Because the brain finds its way to negativity three times easier, it is likely to label an event as negative, more often than positive or neutral.

The real question is: how can our brain instantly label an event negative? Most of the time, we can only determine whether an event was positive or negative after the fact. Let's say your friend gets fired. Right then, the subconscious slaps a negative label on the event. A few weeks later, she discovers her professional calling in another arena. She has never been happier. This obviously changes the event label from negative to positive.

Can you see why it is wiser for the brain to start with a neutral label, while it waits to make its final label choice further down the track?

Exercise:

Disrupt this negative classification process going on in your subconscious brain. Every time the subconscious brain classifies an event as negative, recognize it. Please don't ignore it. Consciously refuse to accept the event as negative, and classify it as being neutral for the time being. Write the event down in your book. Write the date 14 days from now, and make an appointment with your brain to formally label this event then. When the date comes, check the label, and adjust as necessary.

S. How to apply in actual practice

By now, you are already experiencing some big changes in your life. The power of your personal development lies in recognition, repetition and continuation. Stick with your exercises, and reap the rewards. You're not finished yet!

Sharing with others is both caring, and personal recognition. Therefore, we have created an international community for "SparkWisers" on Facebook.

As a reader of our book, you are more than welcome to join and share your experiences, tips, tricks and information. Post questions, or help others find their personal answers. Above all, show respect for each other.

Please try to search for <u>similarities</u> in remarks others make, <u>instead of differences</u>. We all carry the burden of a pre-programmed archive created in our past. Beware of the pitfall of the strong, negative, fear-driven search for differences.

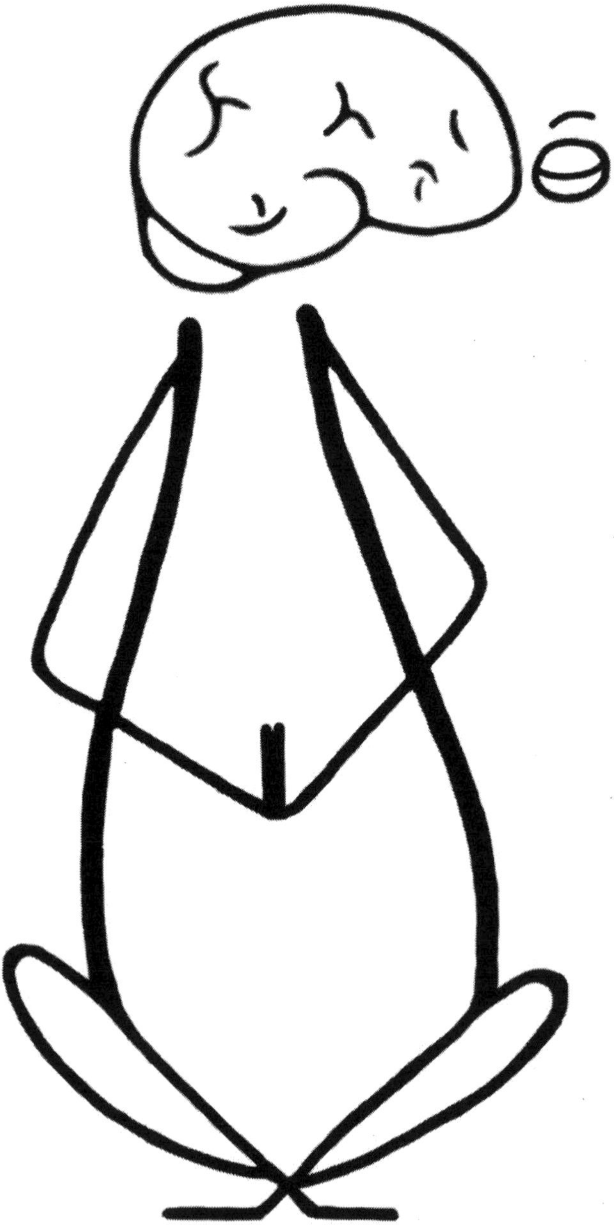

23. SparkWise Quotes

Feel free to customize, personalize, and share the quotes you like most on social media.

SparkWise Quote:
"Knowing and understanding the cause, is the essential key to changing the effects and becoming brilliant"

SparkWise Quote:
"When we learn to understand how the brain operates, we can enhance the quality of all decisions"

SparkWise Quote:
"What is the truth? A perceived mixture of DNA, childhood, and further education by believing the truth of others?"

SparkWise Quote:
"Our protective fear system activates the natural resistance against any form of change"

SparkWise Quote:
"Our well-equipped subconscious worked well in nature, but does not operate so well in our today's concrete Urban jungle"

SparkWise Quote:
"Subconscious determination conflicts with rational thinking, while intelligence at the same time is certain it considered all possibilities."

SparkWise Quote:
"By understanding how to eat excellent for our brain cells, we provide our body with more energy"

SparkWise Quote:
"The fundamental distinction between asking for intrinsic motivation and activating intrinsic motivation, is knowing which hormones to switch on"

SparkWise Quote:
"The new leading by example is not telling somebody what to do, but asking how they would deal with it"

SparkWise Quote:
"Time is precious to the brain. Sending somebody an E-mail is no time priority for the brain. Walking to somebody's desk and asking for help how to solve a challenge is"

SparkWise Quote:
"Fiction and reality is almost the same for the brain. Use gamification to reduce primary resistance in rapid changing environments"

SparkWise Quote:
"Make use of the natural positive peer group pressure, to stimulate and activate a cycle of positive behavior among the individuals of the group"

SparkWise Quote:
"Holding on to self-determination is a necessity to establish inner balance and becoming happy and successful"

SparkWise Quote:
"To avoid lengthy emotional discussions with someone angry: say their first name, ask a topic related question, stop for a second, and present two answer options. Do you mean A… or do you mean B….? Repeat the process"

SparkWise Quote:
"Humanity lacks general brain knowledge. Only by improving individual brain knowledge, humans can transform and become successful"

SparkWise Quote:
"Giving a present to someone is rated three times higher by our brain, than receiving a present from someone"

24. Research and references combined

Adam, T. C., and E. S. Epel. "Stress, Eating and the Reward System." Physiology & Behavior. July 24, 2007. https://www.ncbi.nlm.nih.gov/pubmed/17543357

Adrien, J. "Neurobiological Bases for the Relation between Sleep and Depression." Sleep Medicine Reviews. October 2002. https://www.ncbi.nlm.nih.gov/pubmed/12531125.

Amen, Daniel. "Brain Health Tips from Dr. Daniel Amen - SuperheroYou." YouTube. October 08, 2012. https://www.youtube.com/watch?v=nMzi0kvcKR0.

American Heart Association. "HDL (Good), LDL (Bad) Cholesterol and Triglycerides." Heart.org. Accessed November 08, 2013. http://www.heart.org/HEARTORG/Conditions/Cholesterol/HDLLDLTriglycerides/HDL-Good-LDL-Bad-Cholesterol-and-Triglycerides_UCM_305561_Article.jsp#.WW4ju4TyiM8.

Anderson, B., and T. Harvey. "Alterations in Cortical Thickness and Neuronal Density in the Frontal Cortex of Albert Einstein." Neuroscience Letters. June 07, 1996. https://www.ncbi.nlm.nih.gov/pubmed/8805120.

Asprey, Dave. *The Bulletproof Diet: Lose up to a Pound a Day, Reclaim Your Energy and Focus, and Upgrade Your Life*. Emmaus, PA: Rodale Books, 2014.

Auer, D. P., B. Pütz, E. Kraft, B. Lipinski, J. Schill, and F. Holsboer. "Reduced Glutamate in the Anterior Cingulate Cortex in Depression: An in Vivo Proton Magnetic Resonance Spectroscopy Study." Biological Psychiatry. February 15, 2000. https://www.ncbi.nlm.nih.gov/pubmed/10686265.

Banks, W. A., A. B. Coon, S. M. Robinson, A. Moinuddin, J. M. Shultz, R. Nakaoke, and J. E. Morley. "Triglycerides Induce Leptin Resistance at the Blood-brain Barrier." Diabetes. May 2004. https://www.ncbi.nlm.nih.gov/pubmed/15111494.

Baumeister, R. F., E. Bratslavsky, M. Muraven, and D. M. Tice. "Ego Depletion: Is the Active Self a Limited Resource?" Journal of Personality and Social Psychology. May 1998. https://www.ncbi.nlm.nih.gov/pubmed/9599441.

Baumeister, Roy F., Ellen Bratslavsky, Catrin Finkenauer, and Kathleen D. Vohs. "Bad Is Stronger than Good." *Review of General Psychology* 5, no. 4 (2001): 323-70.

Becker, Kirk A. "History of the Stanford-Binet Intelligence Scales: Content and Psychometrics." Hmhco.com. 2003. http://www.hmhco.com/~/media/sites/home/hmh-assessments/clinical/stanford-binet/pdf/sb5_asb_1.pdf?la=en.

Beyerstein, Barry L. "Do We Really Use Only 10 Percent of Our Brains?" Scientific American. Accessed November 11, 2014. https://www.scientificamerican.com/article/do-we-really-use-only-10/.

Blinkov, Samuil M., Il'ia I. Glezer, and Basil Haigh. *The Human Brain in Figures and Tables: A Quantitative Handbook*. New York: Basic Books, 1968.

Bohórquez, Diego V., Rafiq A. Shahid, Alan Erdmann, Alex M. Kreger, Yu Wang, Nicole Calakos, Fan Wang, and Rodger A. Liddle. "Neuroepithelial Circuit Formed by Innervation of Sensory Enteroendocrine Cells." The Journal of Clinical Investigation. February 2, 2015. Accessed August 18, 2015. https://www.jci.org/articles/view/78361/pdf.

Boring, Ronald L. "Fifty Years of THERP and Human Reliability Analysis." *INL* PSAM11 (June 2012). https://inldigitallibrary.inl.gov/sites/sti/sti/5680968.pdf.

Bowles, Samuel, and Herbert Gintis. *A Cooperative Species: Human Reciprocity and Its Evolution*. Princeton, NJ: Princeton Univ. Press, 2013.

Brown, Frank, John Fleagle, and Ian McDougall. "The Oldest Homo Sapiens." University of Utah News. February 2005. https://archive.unews.utah.edu/news_releases/the-oldest-homo-sapiens.

Brown, Richard E. "Hebb and Cattell: The Genesis of the Theory of Fluid and Crystallized Intelligence." Frontiers in Human Neuroscience. 2016. https://www.ncbi.nlm.nih.gov/pmc/articles/PMC5156710/.

Burnett, Dean. *Idiot Brain*. London: Guardian Faber Publishing, 2016.

Campbell, A. "Oxytocin and Human Social Behavior." Personality and Social Psychology Review : An Official Journal of the Society for Personality and Social Psychology, Inc. August 2010.https://www.ncbi.nlm.nih.gov/pubmed/20435805

Cattell, Raymond B. "Fluid Intelligence versus Crystallized Intelligence." PsycNET. Accessed January, 2013. http://dx.doi.org/10.1037/h0046743.

Chapman, S. B., S. Aslan, J. S. Spence, L. F. Defina, M. W. Keebler, N. Didehbani, and H. Lu. "Shorter Term Aerobic Exercise Improves Brain, Cognition, and Cardiovascular Fitness in Aging." Frontiers in Aging Neuroscience. November 12, 2013.https://www.ncbi.nlm.nih.gov/pubmed/24282403.

Charvet, C. J., and B. L. Finlay. "Embracing Covariation in Brain Evolution: Large Brains, Extended Development, and Flexible Primate Social Systems." Progress in Brain Research. Accessed November 08, 2016. https://www.ncbi.nlm.nih.gov/pubmed/22230623.

Cialdini, Robert B., Joyce E. Vincent, Stephen K. Lewis, Jose Catalan, Diane Wheeler, and Betty Lee Darby. "Reciprocal Concessions Procedure for Inducing Compliance: The Door-in-the-face Technique." *Journal of Personality and Social Psychology* 31, no. 2 (1975): 206-15. doi:10.1037/h0076284.

Confucius. "Confucius Quotes." BrainyQuote. Accessed January 20, 2015. https://www.brainyquote.com/quotes/quotes/c/confucius134717.html.

Cowan, N. "The Magical Number 4 in Short-term Memory: A Reconsideration of Mental Storage Capacity." The Behavioral and Brain Sciences. February 2001. https://www.ncbi.nlm.nih.gov/pubmed/11515286.

Deary, I. J., S. Strand, P. Smith, and C. Fernandes. "Intelligence and Educational Achievement." Intelligence. March 06, 2006. http://www.sciencedirect.com/science/article/pii/S0160289606000171.

Dedovic, K., A. Duchesne, J. Andrews, V. Engert, and J. C. Pruessner. "The Brain and the Stress Axis: The Neural Correlates of Cortisol Regulation in Response to Stress." NeuroImage. September 2009. https://www.ncbi.nlm.nih.gov/pubmed/19500680.

Diamond, M. C., A. B. Scheibel, J. R. Murphy, and T. Harvey. "On the Brain of a Scientist: Albert Einstein." Experimental Neurology. April 1985. Accessed December 09, 2015. https://www.ncbi.nlm.nih.gov/pubmed/3979509.

Dispenza, Joe, and Daniel G. Amen. *Breaking the Habit of Being Yourself: How to Lose Your Mind and Create a New One*. Carlsbad, CA: Hay House, 2015.

Dispenza, Joe. *You Are the Placebo: Making Your Mind Matter*. Carlsbad, CA: Hay House, 2015.

Dávid-Barrett, T., and R. I. M. Dunbar. "Processing Power Limits Social Group Size: Computational Evidence for the Cognitive Costs of Sociality." Proceedings of the Royal Society B: Biological Sciences. August 22, 2013. https://www.ncbi.nlm.nih.gov/pmc/articles/PMC3712454/.

Dweck, Carol. S. *Mindset: The New Psychology of Success*. New York: Ballantine Books, 2007.

Dweck, Carol S. "The Secret to Raising Smart Kids." Scientific American. January 01, 2015. https://www.scientificamerican.com/article/the-secret-to-raising-smart-kids1/.

Eichenbaum, Howard. *The Cognitive Neuroscience of Memory: An Introduction*. New York, N.Y.: Oxford Univ. Press, 2002.

Einstein, Albert. "Albert Einstein Quotes." BrainyQuote. Accessed September 06, 2015. https://www.brainyquote.com/quotes/authors/a/albert_einstein.html.

Eyre, H., and B. T. Baune. "Neuroplastic Changes in Depression: A Role for the Immune System." Psychoneuroendocrinology. September 2012. https://www.ncbi.nlm.nih.gov/pubmed/22525700.

Gaby, A. R. "Adverse Effects of Dietary Fructose." Alternative Medicine Review : A Journal of Clinical Therapeutic. December 2005. https://www.ncbi.nlm.nih.gov/pubmed/16366738.

Gandhi, Mahatma. "Mahatma Gandhi Quotes." BrainyQuote. Accessed October 04, 2015. https://www.brainyquote.com/quotes/authors/m/mahatma_gandhi.html.

Garfield, A. S., C. Li, J. C. Madara, B. P. Shah, E. Webber, J. S. Steger, J. N. Campbell, O. Gavrilova, C. E. Lee, D. P. Olson, J. K. Elmquist, B. A. Tannous, M. J. Krashes, and B. B. Lowell. "A Neural Basis for Melanocortin-4 Receptor-regulated Appetite." Nature Neuroscience. June 2015. https://www.ncbi.nlm.nih.gov/pubmed/25915476.

Harris, S., J. T. Kaplan, A. Curiel, S. Y. Bookheimer, M. Iacoboni, and M. S. Cohen. "The Neural Correlates of Religious and Nonreligious Belief." PloS One. October 01, 2009. https://www.ncbi.nlm.nih.gov/pubmed/19794914.

Harvard Health Publishing. "What Causes Depression?" Harvard Health Publishing. June 2009. Accessed April 17, 2017. https://www.health.harvard.edu/mind-and-mood/what-causes-depression.

Hewitt, Michael. "Sun, Sea and Shrinking Brain Power." The Telegraph. August 15, 2011. http://www.telegraph.co.uk/news/health/news/8698244/Sun-sea-and-shrinking-brain-power.html.

Hoeft, F., C. L. Watson, S. R. Kesler, K. E. Bettinger, and A. L. Reiss. "Gender Differences in the Mesocorticolimbic System during Computer Game-play." Journal of Psychiatric Research. March 2008. https://www.ncbi.nlm.nih.gov/pubmed/18194807.

Hof, Wim. "Van Circusartiest "Iceman" Naar Wetenschap "Wim Hof"." Innerfire - Extraordinary in Everyone. Accessed July 21, 2017. http://www.innerfire.nl/.

Jobs, Steve. "Steve Jobs Quotes." BrainyQuote. Accessed November 03, 2013. https://www.brainyquote.com/quotes/quotes/s/stevejobs416859.html.

Johnson, W. G. "The Management Oversight and Risk Tree -mort: Including Systems Developed Idaho Operations Office and Aerojet Nuclear Company." MORT. February 12, 1973. http://www.nri.eu.com/SAN8212.pdf.

Jones, E., and A. Symes. "Leptin and TGF-beta Synergistically Regulate VIP Cytokine Response Element Transcription." Neuroreport. December 18, 2000. https://www.ncbi.nlm.nih.gov/pubmed/11192627.

Kahneman, Daniel. *Thinking, Fast and Slow*. Amsterdam: Uitgeverij Business Contact, 2011.

Kallen, Victor. "Hoe Stress in Je Brein Je Prestatie En Gezondheid Bepalen." TNO. Accessed September 18, 2015. https://www.tno.nl/nl/aandachtsgebieden/defensie-veiligheid/human-effectiveness/hoe-stress-in-je-brein-je-prestatie-en-gezondheid-bepalen/.

Karwowski, Waldemar. *International Encyclopedia of Ergonomics and Human Factors*. London: Taylor & Francis, 2006.

Kazén, M., T. Kuenne, H. Frankenberg, and M. Quirin. "Inverse Relation between Cortisol and Anger and Their Relation to Performance and Explicit Memory." Biological Psychology. September 2012. https://www.ncbi.nlm.nih.gov/pubmed/22627590.

Keys, Ancel. "The Seven Countries Study - Study Findings." Seven Countries Study | The First Study to Relate Diet with Cardiovascular Disease. 1958. http://www.sevencountriesstudy.com/study-findings.

Killingsworth, M. A., and D. T. Gilbert. "A Wandering Mind Is an Unhappy Mind." Science (New York, N.Y.). November 12, 2010. https://www.ncbi.nlm.nih.gov/pubmed/21071660.

Kross, E., M. G. Berman, W. Mischel, E. E. Smith, and T. D. Wager. "Social Rejection Shares Somatosensory Representations with Physical Pain." Proceedings of the National Academy of Sciences of the United States of America. April 12, 2011. https://www.ncbi.nlm.nih.gov/pubmed/21444827.

LeDoux, J. "The Amygdala." Current Biology : CB. October 23, 2007. https://www.ncbi.nlm.nih.gov/pubmed/17956742.

Leheska, J. M., L. D. Thompson, J. C. Howe, E. Hentges, J. Boyce, J. C. Brooks, B. Shriver, L. Hoover, and M. F. Miller. "Effects of Conventional and Grass-feeding Systems on the Nutrient Composition of Beef." Journal of Animal Science. December 2008. https://www.ncbi.nlm.nih.gov/pubmed/18641180.

Lindeman, Marjaana, Annika M. Svedholm, Tapani Riekki, Tuukka Raij, and Riitta Hari. "Is It Just a Brick Wall or a Sign from the Universe? An FMRI Study of Supernatural Believers and Skeptics." Social Cognitive and Affective Neuroscience. December 2013. https://www.ncbi.nlm.nih.gov/pmc/articles/PMC3831561/.

Lipton, Bruce H. *The Biology of Belief: Unleashing the Power of Consciousness, Matter & Miracles*. Carlsbad, CA: Hay House, 2016.

Lipton, Bruce H. "Using 100 percent of Your Brain - Dr. Bruce H. Lipton." YouTube. May 08, 2015. https://www.youtube.com/watch?v=4ZNi68xVDWU.

Martin, Steve J., Noah J. Goldstein, and Robert B. Cialdini. *The Small BIG: Small Changes That Spark BIG Influence*. London: Profile Books, 2015.

McConnell, Alison. *Breathe Strong, Perform Better*. Champaign, IL: Human Kinetics, 2011.

McGuigan, Lauren E. "Cognitive Effects of Alcohol Abuse." Wichita State University. 2011. http://soar.wichita.edu/bitstream/handle/10057/6827/t13029_McGuigan.pdf;sequence=1.

McKay, Sarah. "7 Daily Habits of Highly Effective Brains." Your Brain Health. Accessed December 12, 2016. http://yourbrainhealth.com.au/.

Mckee, Ann C., Robert C. Cantu, Christopher J. Nowinski, E. Tessa Hedley-Whyte, Brandon E. Gavett, Andrew E. Budson, Veronica E. Santini, Hyo-Soon Lee, Caroline A. Kubilus, and Robert A. Stern. "Chronic Traumatic Encephalopathy in Athletes: Progressive Tauopathy After Repetitive Head Injury." *Journal of Neuropathology & Experimental Neurology* 68, no. 7 (2009): 709-35. doi:10.1097/nen.0b013e3181a9d503.

Milgram, S. "Behavioral study of obedience." Journal of Abnormal Psychology. October 1963. https://www.ncbi.nlm.nih.gov/pubmed/14049516.

Milner, David, and Melvyn A. Goodale. *The Visual Brain in Action*. Oxford: Oxford University Press, 1995.

Miyake, Akira, and Naomi P. Friedman. "The Nature and Organization of Individual Differences in Executive Functions: Four General Conclusions." Current Directions in Psychological Science. February 2012. https://www.ncbi.nlm.nih.gov/pmc/articles/PMC3388901/.

Morgan, C. A., S. Southwick, G. Steffian, G. A. Hazlett, and E. F. Loftus. "Misinformation Can Influence Memory for Recently Experienced, Highly Stressful Events." International Journal of Law and Psychiatry. 2012. https://www.ncbi.nlm.nih.gov/pubmed/23219699.

Mosley, Michael. "The Second Brain in Our Stomachs." BBC News. July 11, 2012. http://www.bbc.com/news/health-18779997.

Mullainathan, Sendhil, and Eldar Shafir. *Scarcity: The New Science of Having Less and How It Defines Our Lives*. New York: Picador/Henry Holt and Company, 2014.

National Human Genome Research Institute (NHGRI). Accessed December 08, 2015. https://www.genome.gov/.

Neuroscapelab. "Glass Brain Flythrough." YouTube. March 01, 2014. https://www.youtube.com/watch?v=dAIQeTeMJ-I.

Newton, Isaac, and N. W. Chittenden. *Newton's Principia: The Mathematical Principles of Natural Philosophy*. Whitefish, MT: Kessinger Publishing, 1687.

Pakkenberg, B. "Aging and the Human Neocortex." *Experimental Gerontology* 38, no. 1-2 (2003): 95-99. doi:10.1016/s0531-5565(02)00151-1.

Perlmutter, David, and Kristin Loberg. *Grain Brain: The Surprising Truth about Wheat, Carbs, and Sugar - Your Brain's Silent Killers*. London: Hodder & Stoughton, 2014.

Pope, Devin G., and Maurice E. Schweitzer. "Is Tiger Woods Loss Averse? Persistent Bias in the Face of Experience, Competition, and High Stakes." *American Economic Review* 101, no. 1 (2011): 129-57. doi:10.1257/aer.101.1.129.

Raichle, Marcus E. "Appraising the Brain's Energy Budget." Proceedings of the National Academy of Sciences. 2002. Accessed April 10, 2012. http://www.pnas.org/content/99/16/10237.full.

Rácz, Gábor. "Explaining the Accelerating Expansion of the Universe without Dark Energy." ScienceDaily. March 30, 2017. https://www.sciencedaily.com/releases/2017/03/170330115254.htm.

Roese, Neal J. "Counterfactual Thinking." *Psychological Bulletin: American Pyschological Association* 121, no. 1 (1997): 133-48. http://www2.psych.ubc.ca/~schaller/Psyc590Readings/Roese1997.pdf.

Ryan, R. M., and E. L. Deci. "Self-determination Theory and the Facilitation of Intrinsic Motivation, Social Development, and Well-being." The American Psychologist. January 2000. https://www.ncbi.nlm.nih.gov/pubmed/11392867.

Schlaug, G., L. Jäncke, Y. Huang, J. F. Staiger, and H. Steinmetz. "Increased Corpus Callosum Size in Musicians." Neuropsychologia. August 1995. https://www.ncbi.nlm.nih.gov/pubmed/8524453.

Shorrock, Steven, and Barry Kirwan. "Technique For The Retrospective And Predictive Analysis Of Cognitive Error (TRACEr and TRACEr-lite)." FAA - Human Factors Division. Accessed November 08, 2017. http://www.hf.faa.gov/workbenchtools/default.aspx?rPage=Tooldetails&subCatId=42&toolID=267.

Studer-Rohr, I., D. R. Dietrich, J. Schlatter, and C. Schlatter. "The Occurrence of Ochratoxin A in Coffee." Food and Chemical Toxicology : An International Journal Published for the British Industrial Biological Research Association. May 1995. https://www.ncbi.nlm.nih.gov/pubmed/7759018.

Swaab, Dick F. *We Are Our Brains: From the Womb to Alzheimer's*. London: Penguin Books, 2015.

Swain, A. D. "Accident Sequence Evaluation Program: Human Reliability Analysis Procedure." 1987. doi:10.2172/6370593.

Taki, Y., H. Hashizume, Y. Sassa, H. Takeuchi, M. Asano, K. Asano, Y. Kotozaki, R. Nouchi, K. Wu, H. Fukuda, and R. Kawashima. "Correlation among Body Height, Intelligence, and Brain Gray Matter Volume in Healthy Children." NeuroImage. January 16, 2012. https://www.ncbi.nlm.nih.gov/pubmed/21930215.

Talsma, Annet, and Martin De Munnik. *De Koopknop: Het Geheim Van Het Consumentenbrein: Inclusief Meer Dan 50 Neuromarketingtips*. Den Haag: Academic Service, 2012.

Thaler, Richard H., and Cass R. Sunstein. *Nudge: Improving Decisions about Health, Wealth, and Happiness*. New York: Penguin Books, 2009.

Todorov, A., A. N. Mandisodza, A. Goren, and C. C. Hall. "Inferences of Competence from Faces Predict Election Outcomes." Science (New York, N.Y.). June 10, 2005. https://www.ncbi.nlm.nih.gov/pubmed/15947187.

Todorov, Alexander, Sean G. Baron, and Nikolaas N. Oosterhof. "Evaluating Face Trustworthiness: A Model Based Approach." Social Cognitive and Affective Neuroscience. June 2008.https://www.ncbi.nlm.nih.gov/pmc/articles/PMC2555464/.

Tononi, G., and C. Cirelli. "Perchance to Prune. During Sleep, the Brain Weakens the Connections among Nerve Cells, Apparently Conserving Energy And, Paradoxically, Aiding Memory." Scientific American. August 2013. https://www.ncbi.nlm.nih.gov/pubmed/23923204.

Turella, L., A. C. Pierno, F. Tubaldi, and U. Castiello. "Mirror Neurons in Humans: Consisting or Confounding Evidence?" Brain and Language. January 2009. https://www.ncbi.nlm.nih.gov/pubmed/18082250.

Tversky, A., and D. Kahneman. "The Framing of Decisions and the Psychology of Choice." Science (New York, N.Y.). January 30, 1981. https://www.ncbi.nlm.nih.gov/pubmed/7455683.

Ulrich, R. S., R. F. Simons, B. D. Losito, E. Fiorito, M. A. Miles, and M. Zelson. "Stress Recovery during Exposure to Natural and Urban Environments." Journal of Environmental Psychology. July 08, 2005. http://www.sciencedirect.com/science/article/pii/S0272494405801847.

"Use Your Biological Strengths to Enhance Professional Success, DNA Research and Assessments." BrainCompass | An Innovative Assessment Platform for Professionals. Accessed May 13, 2017. http://www.braincompass.com/en/.

Van den Bos, E., and P. M. Westenberg. "Two-year Stability of Individual Differences in (para)sympathetic and HPA-axis Responses to Public Speaking in Childhood and Adolescence." Psychophysiology. March 2015. https://www.ncbi.nlm.nih.gov/pubmed/25267560.

Van den Bos, E., M. De Rooij, A. C. Miers, C. L. Bokhorst, and P. M. Westenberg. "Adolescents' Increasing Stress Response to Social Evaluation: Pubertal Effects on Cortisol and Alpha-amylase during Public Speaking." Child Development. 2014. https://www.ncbi.nlm.nih.gov/pubmed/23638912.

Van den Bos, E., M. Tops, and P. M. Westenberg. "Social Anxiety and the Cortisol Response to Social Evaluation in Children and Adolescents." Psychoneuroendocrinology. April 2017. https://www.ncbi.nlm.nih.gov/pubmed/28209542.

Watson, Lyall. "Lyall Watson Quotes." BrainyQuote. Accessed August 14, 2015. https://www.brainyquote.com/quotes/authors/l/lyall_watson.html.

Whalen, Paul J., Hannah Raila, Randi Bennett, Alison Mattek, Annemarie Brown, James Taylor, Michelle Van Tieghem, Alexandra Tanner, Matthew Miner, and Amy Palmer. "Neuroscience and Facial Expressions of Emotion: The Role of Amygdala—Prefrontal Interactions." *Emotion Review* 5, no. 1 (2013): 78-83. doi:10.1177/1754073912457231.

Williams, J. C. "Human Error Assessment and Reduction Technique (HEART)." *Incident Investigation and Accident Prevention in the Process and Allied Industries*, 2006. doi:10.1201/9781439822449.axh.

Witelson, Sandra F. "How Albert Einstein's Brain Worked." Accessed October 12, 2015. Michael G. De Groot School of Medicine.

SPARKWISE

Printed in Germany
by Amazon
Distribution